GIDON LEV WITH JULIE GRAY

LET'S MAKE THINGS BETTER

A Holocaust Survivor's Message of Hope and Celebration of Life

hachette
BOOKS

New York

Hachette Go, an imprint of Hachette Books
Hachette Book Group
1290 Avenue of the Americas
New York, NY 10104
HachetteGo.com
Facebook.com/HachetteGo
Instagram.com/HachetteGo

First Edition: November 2024

Published by Hachette Go, an imprint of Hachette Book Group, Inc. The Hachette Go name and logo are trademarks of the Hachette Book Group.

The Hachette Speakers Bureau provides a wide range of authors for speaking events. To find out more, visit hachettespeakersbureau.com or email HachetteSpeakers@hbgusa.com.

Hachette Go books may be purchased in bulk for business, educational, or promotional use. For information, please contact your local bookseller or email the Hachette Book Group Special Markets Department at Special.Markets@hbgusa.com.

The publisher is not responsible for websites (or their content) that are not owned by the publisher.

Library of Congress Cataloging-in-Publication Data

Names: Lev, Gidon, 1935– author; Gray, Julie, 1964– author
Title: Let's make things better: a holocaust survivor's message of hope and
    celebration of life / Gidon Lev, with Julie Gray.
Description: First edition. | New York, NY: Hachette Go, 2024.
Identifiers: LCCN 2024012557 | ISBN 9780306835636 (hardcover) |
    ISBN 9780306835643 (paperback) | ISBN 9780306835650 (ebook)
Subjects: LCSH: Lev, Gidon, 1935– | Theresienstadt (Concentration camp) |
    Holocaust, Jewish (1939–1945)—Czechoslovakia—Personal narratives |
    Holocaust survivors—Israel—Biography. | Jewish children in the
    Holocaust—Czechoslovakia—Biography. | Lev, Gidon, 1935–—Family. |
    Karlovy Vary (Czech Republic)—Biography.
Classification: LCC DS135.C97 L478 2024 | DDC
    940.53/18092—dc23/eng/20240529
LC record available at https://lccn.loc.gov/2024012557

ISBNs: 978-0-306-83563-6 (hardcover) 978-0-306-83565-0 (ebook)

Printed in the United States of America

LSC-C

Printing 1, 2024

To anyone in the world—whatever their gender, color, or religious beliefs—who needs a reminder that, in spite of past or even present suffering, life is wonderful and full of adventures and opportunities. So let's make things better!

CONTENTS

Gidon in Tel Aviv.

INTRODUCTION

Gidon Lev, the little boy who never quite grew up, is taking a nap inside a sun-bleached cabin a few kilometers from the Egyptian border in the Negev desert. The dusty wind whistles in the cracks of our cabin and rustles the palm fronds on the roof. Gidon sports the orange, blue, and green madras shirt he picked out from a secondhand shop a few days ago. He also came home with some chairs for the dining table and a ladle. Shimon Peres once stayed in this cabin, or so we are told.

Tomorrow we will celebrate Gidon's eighty-ninth birthday, and I've brought him down into the desert for his annual birthday surprise. In birthdays past, we have gone ziplining, up in a hot-air balloon, and indoor skydiving, to name a few. So far, Gidon has no idea what we'll be doing tomorrow, but as usual, he is game.

As is my habit, as Gidon lies there sleeping, which is the only time he is still, I watch his chest to make sure it's rising and falling. He has been slowing down a lot lately. Nine decades of a life well and truly lived will do that to you.

I try not to think too often about the fact that Gidon is on loan to me for a very short time, but this, of course, is something I cannot ignore. I have tried to prepare myself for Life Without Gidon, but I'm not sure there will be any soft landing after having been swept up in his wonderful orbit for as long as I have. Yet Gidon has left me changed—and not left me yet. I don't think he ever really will.

On the eve of his ninetieth journey around the sun, I wonder to myself for the millionth time, What animates this man, this Gidon Lev? What has brought him and I, this odd couple, to this very moment, on a goat farm in the middle of the desert? How did I get here?

Suddenly, Gidon opens one blue eye and smiles at me impishly. "Aha!" He laughs, pleased that he startled me.

•◆•

In the fall of 2017, an elderly man called me up out of the blue and said he needed someone to help him write a book. He was a Holocaust survivor, he explained, and he wanted to tell the stories of his life. Could I help him? Could I meet him for a cup of coffee? I said yes.

Like most of the ordinary yet potentially life-changing moments of our lives, I had no idea what that single word, that *yes*, portended.

From that cup of coffee onward, Gidon Lev has merrily proceeded to reroute the trajectory of my life.

•◆•

When I met Gidon, I was unsuccessfully trying to do an Eat Pray Love, that is, "reinvent" myself in an exotic place. In 2010, I lost my brother to suicide, and I was cast utterly adrift. Drowning in grief, I thought it would be a pretty good idea to move from Los Angeles to Israel. I didn't speak a word of

Hebrew. Sad Incompetent American Lady wasn't really on my bingo card after what I'd been through, but there you go.

What followed were a few valiant years of volunteering, writing, making new friends, and speaking in a strange and, I am sure, quite comical patois of English and Hebrew. I got by. But I also discovered that you can't outrun grief. I didn't realize it yet, but I needed a partner in life, someone with whom I could feel safe enough to explore my grief and maybe—just maybe—even restore a sense of purpose and hope.

Over our first cup of coffee, Gidon Lev upended my preconceived notions about Holocaust survivors, not to mention elderly people. He then proceeded to challenge what I thought of as the conventions of polite conversation. He was very curious; he wanted to know all about me, why I was in Israel, what had happened to my brother, and how I was dealing with it. Gidon was, he explained, passionate about people expressing themselves honestly and getting right down to the heart of things. Somehow, Gidon's unapologetic frankness made me feel safe.

It was clear to me that I had met an inveterate raconteur and a human dynamo who loved nothing more than to make good trouble. Reader, he had me at *shalom*.

•◆•

It didn't take very long for us to realize that we were two peas in a pod. It was everything from our shared values about the five-second rule to fork sharing to our mutual love of Simon & Garfunkel that bound us together very quickly. A few months after we met, we moved in together and then we wrote *The*

True Adventures of Gidon Lev: Rascal. Holocaust Survivor. Optimist. I was Gidon's girlfriend, his main squeeze, his editor, and his manager. And he was the chief gravy maker, my ad hoc therapist, and my rock.

•—•

Since that single *yes* and that fated cup of coffee many years ago, Gidon and I have traveled the world and met very many stern dignitaries in European cities. We have laid wreaths and we have gotten lost in airports and we have argued in the pasta and rice aisle at the grocery store. We once both fell through a cattle grate—simultaneously—late at night outside a farm in the Golan Heights. Don't ask.

I have come to learn that Gidon is like his own mischievous weather system—I just hang on for dear life and follow in his wake, sometimes apologizing and very often paying for parking tickets.

•—•

By far, my favorite moments with Gidon, the ones that endear him to me most, are the small moments, just between us. Like the time he whooshed up in his beat-up Suzuki Splash to pick me up, honking and waving cheerfully. "Gidon—did you eat spaghetti for lunch?" I asked. His mouth was ringed with faint remnants of spaghetti sauce. "Yep," Gidon said. And off we sped.

Or the time when I was quietly working on my computer when, suddenly, there was an ear-splitting wrenching sound from somewhere in the house. Gidon had decided to take the door off our bathroom to get our new washing machine to fit through. While I surveyed the devastation and looked at him incredulously, Gidon simply explained, from where he was on the floor with a crowbar, that no, the door probably couldn't really be put back on again, but not to worry, he planned to put a shower curtain up in its place.

Or when, despite my by then feeble protestations, he tied a thick branch, at least five feet long, to the back of our car and dragged it at least a mile down a dirt road so we would have wood for our campfire. The branch wound up puncturing our oil pan, something we did not discover until the following day, when we also discovered that we had set up camp next to a popular hiking path. We must have looked ridiculous in our camping pajamas peering at the puddle of oil under our car as hikers trekked past.

.•.

Gidon Lev is a sprite, a rascal, and sometimes, yes, even a royal pain in the behind. No, Gidon, a shower curtain is not a good substitute for a door. Yet Gidon's unfettered, unfiltered, and irrepressible soul is simply irresistible to me. And clearly to many others.

Not infrequently, Gidon is recognized for having been on television or from his social media accounts. He has quite an effect on people. Recently, a woman in a café in Kraków clapped her hand over her mouth when she saw him. Most people ask to take a selfie with him. Sometimes people hug him and cry. All this, Gidon, the little boy who never quite grew up, takes in stride.

I have often wondered how a man whose childhood was so totally, brutally opposite from my own can possibly be so relentlessly cheerful. Yet, suffering is relative, as Gidon would be the first to say. Loneliness can be a piercing experience, and you need not be in a concentration camp to feel it. There are a thousand and one varieties of suffering in this world; Gidon does not consider himself to be the arbiter or prime example of pain. He is wiser and humbler than that. Yet he does recognize his place in history and the responsibility that comes with it.

•—•

I have spent at least ten thousand hours trying to figure out what it is about Gidon that makes him so relentlessly inquisitive, playful, cheerful, and optimistic. Over sixty thousand hours, actually. I can only conclude that Gidon has some kind of magical Vitamin G flowing through his veins. Believe me, I would bottle this if I could.

In my quest to understand what makes Gidon Gidon, I spoke to Oded Adomi Leshem, a PhD, political psychologist, and author of *Hope Amidst Conflict*. Oded told me that it is more likely for those like Gidon, who have gone through unimaginable suffering, to be more hopeful people than those who have not. Hope, Oded explained, is as necessary as food and water. In a brightly lit room, a candle does not make much difference. But when the room is dark, that candle is everything.

Gidon's childhood was spent in the dark. For him, hope is not a cute saying for a coffee cup, T-shirt, or welcome mat. Hope is not aspirational merch. For Gidon, hope is life itself—nonnegotiable.

Beyond Gidon's charming and cheerful demeanor, he is, of course, a complex character. His enthusiastic, all-in nature can, at times, make him a bit reckless, yet he is a deeply wise and patient man too—more than he knows—with depths of compassion and understanding that dwell in his bluest of blue eyes. He is also most decidedly a rascal—a Czech through and through, a man who loves expansively, fails dramatically, and never, ever gives up.

•◆•

We both wanted things to be better while we worked on this book together. It was, in every way, a difficult and even ridiculous time to be working on a book about hope and not giving up. It was a terrifying time to be writing about antisemitism and fake news. Yet it was exactly the right time too. On these pages, Gidon is not musing about hope and making things better from the comfort of time or distance. He is living the urgency of hope in real time.

1

TELLING MY STORY
FOR THE FIRST TIME

Gidon's mother's Star of David.

K ARLOVY VARY IS A HUMBLE LITTLE TOWN NESTLED AMONG FOR-
ested hills and flowing streams. The air is fresh and cold.
In the breeze, there are the fragrances of the forest, pine trees,
and fallen leaves. The beautiful Teplá River runs right through
the middle of town and little bridges cross over it here and
there. There are hot mineral springs too, and people come
from all over Europe to renew their health and spirits in these
waters.

I was born in this wonderful place in 1935. At that time, it was still Czechoslovakia. The home where my family lived is long gone, of course.

Today, when I tell people my story, I always talk about Karlovy Vary first, not because it's where I was born but because that beautiful place is where I would have had a childhood and even grown up had it not been for the war.

.•.•.

It took me over forty years after my liberation from Theresienstadt to be ready to share my story, and when I finally did, it was with the least likely group of people I ever could have imagined—a group of German high school students whose grandparents may very well have been Nazis.

It felt strange, and of course, I was nervous at first, but somehow, finally sharing my memories about my childhood and my family—some of them very painful—was good for me. And I think it was good for the students too. We both had a history to face and to share.

The German students were visiting Israel as part of a "twin city" program. This was in 1985 or so. I do recall that some people in our community were very opposed to this visit; they didn't want Germans in our town because they had suffered terribly at the hands of the Nazis. But the municipality of Nof HaGalil, which is in northern Israel, where I lived, stood its ground. I was happy about that. My thinking was that these are new times with new relationships and we must try to move on.

I became involved with the students' visit because I was teaching Israeli folk dancing at the community center, so the people at the municipality knew me and they knew that I spoke German—maybe not perfectly, but good enough. So they asked me to go along with the German students as they were sightseeing and translate for them. I thought it was a great idea, and I agreed right away. It sounded fun!

The students, their principal, and I traveled together all around the beautiful places in the Galilee region. We went to the Hula Valley, which is a very big nature reserve, where millions of migrating birds land every year, and we went to the Golan Heights. We also showed them all around Lake Kinneret (which is known in the Bible as the Sea of Galilee) and took them to places like Tiberias, Capernaum, and the Mount of Beatitudes. I am sure it was a trip of a lifetime for those students. I loved it, and I loved getting to know them as we traveled around this land that I love. In some ways, it was good for me psychologically to interact with Germans of a new generation.

A couple of days before the students were supposed to go back to Germany, the principal of their school, who had heard that I was a Holocaust survivor, asked me if I would be prepared to talk with the students about my experience during the war. I was a bit nervous about it. I had traveled with and gotten to know the kids a little bit, but I had never told my story to a group before. I didn't know how it would make me feel. But I thought, Well, why not? Jump into it, Gidon Lev!

I simply started at the beginning and told them my story.

•◦•

My father, Arnošt Löw, was born in 1903 in Most, which is not far from Karlovy Vary, in what was known as Bohemia. My father and his father (my grandfather Alfred) owned a scrap iron yard that did very well because, at that time, many new factories opened up, failed, and then had to sell their machinery. My father was introduced to my mother by my great uncle Gustav, who owned a small electrical appliance shop in Karlovy Vary, where my father was a regular client.

My mother, Doris, was born in Karlovy Vary in 1912, but most of her extended family lived in Vienna. My mother's father, Fritz Samish, also lived in Karlovy Vary, with his second wife, Elsa, and their son, Carl Heinz, my mother's half-brother.

My grandfather Fritz had actually served in the army in the First World War, for the Austro-Hungarian Empire. In fact, he was a prisoner of war for over a year on the eastern front. He received a medal of honor from the Austro-Hungarians, which made him feel very secure. He did not think the Germans would ever have anything against him since they were allied with the Austro-Hungarian Empire during that war.

Before the First World War, my grandfather was the manager of a privately owned bank, and he fell in love with the bank owner's daughter, Liesel, who was my grandmother. She was a very lovely, vivacious, outgoing woman. My eldest daughter, Maya, looks a bit like her. In Czech, Liesel's name was Eliška.

Actually, many of my family members had two different names. One in Czech and one in German. So my grandfather's name in Czech was Bedrich, but in German, it was Friedrich, or Fritz for short. My father's Czech name was

4

Arnošt, but it was Ernst in German. My great-grandmother was Ružena but Rosa in German, which means "rose" in both languages.

Because of all this history and sometimes even fighting about what part of the former Austro-Hungarian Empire belonged to whom, I was born in what was called Bohemia by the Czechs, but known as "Sudetenland" to the Germans. In this Sudetenland, there lived many Germans as well as Czechs. There were two cultures, side by side.

All in all, Germans living in Czechoslovakia and their Czech neighbors coexisted peacefully, but there was an underlying tension because many Germans felt that this part of Czechoslovakia really should belong to them. The German culture was somewhat dominant because their numbers were far greater. In my family home, we spoke German, mostly, though we also spoke Czech. German was considered a "higher," more sophisticated language. In fact, I have a very old Jewish prayer book that belonged to one of my great-grandmothers. It was printed in Prague and it's written in German. I think it's amazing, actually, that it's not written in Hebrew or Yiddish or Czech—but German.

•◆•

As I was growing up, I was only vaguely aware of being Jewish. At just three years old, I didn't really know what that meant. We were, for the most part, a secular family, celebrating Hanukkah by lighting the candles, but at the same time we also had a Christmas tree. We celebrated Rosh Hashanah, the Jewish New Year, and observed Yom Kippur, the Day of

Atonement. Most but not all the Jews in Czechoslovakia were secular and integrated into the existing society.

Though I have only a few brief memories of my life in Karlovy Vary before the war, the fragments I do remember, I cherish very much. I do remember that a big German shepherd dog guarded my family's scrap iron yard. One day, I came too close to him. My mother warned me and took my hand. That dog barked and barked and scared me to bits! I also remember sitting at the table and my mother would bring me a small porcelain egg cup that had the figure of a rabbit attached to it. I loved the soft-boiled egg as much as I loved the cup itself; the rabbit looked a bit like an Easter Bunny. And I remember my beautiful red tricycle with black handlebars. It was my third birthday present, and I rode it all the time. My mother would say, "Do you want to ride it into your bed?" I thought, I wish I could!

But, suddenly, in September 1938, everything changed. Adolf Hitler, British prime minister Neville Chamberlain, Italy's fascist leader Benito Mussolini, and Édouard Daladier, the French prime minister, signed the Munich Agreement. Hitler wanted to annex the Sudetenland to Greater Germany. Because Hitler did not recognize the existence of Czechoslovakia, there were no Czech representatives at the meeting.

My family could not have known that this was the beginning of the end. I sometimes wonder how different life would have been for me if that had never happened. To this day, I feel angry and betrayed by the world, but especially Britain and France, who thought that if they gave Hitler the Sudeten, that would appease him. Shortly after the agreement was signed, the Wehrmacht, the German army, entered Czechoslovakia without firing a single shot because the Czech army was told to put down their arms as part of the agreement.

Chamberlain, who had witnessed the horrors of the First World War, wanted to prevent another war at all costs. But in order to do so, he had to close his eyes, ears, and brain because everyone knew that the German war industry was churning out arms and munitions at double and triple time, and not for defense, since no one was threatening Germany, not even the Russians in the east.

Immediately after the Munich Agreement, Jews in the Sudetenland were targeted. They were fired from all municipal positions. Teachers, doctors, lawyers—all lost their jobs. There were lootings and pogroms. The synagogue in Karlovy Vary was burned down. The fact is, during this time late in 1938, the Germans made it impossible for the Jews in the Sudeten to live any kind of normal existence. No Jew felt safe. Jews had no right to work and no right to sell, to buy, or to trade. In short, the Jews of Sudeten had no rights and no future. There was so much uncertainty, fear, and violence.

Being three years old, I of course did not know what was going on. The nanny who looked after me refused to work for us anymore because we were Jews. Or maybe she was scared to work for us. I will never really know. Anyway, she left and that was the end of that.

My family and many others decided to flee to Prague, thinking that it would be a safe haven for Jews. After all, it was still democratic Czechoslovakia. But that was foolish and wishful thinking. About two thousand Jewish people escaped

Karlovy Vary during that time, including my family. After the war, only about twenty-five of us would return.

It was late at night when we left Karlovy Vary. It was me, my mother and father, and my grandma Theresie and grandpa Alfred. There was a night train from Karlovy Vary to Prague, which was about an hour and a half away. I remember that it was a cool night. We had as many of our things as we could carry, suitcases, bedrolls, and knapsacks. Of course, I had my beloved red tricycle with me. But as we got on the train, suddenly (or so it seemed to me) my parents said that I could not take my tricycle with me because we had too many things and it just wouldn't fit. For me, this was a devasting pronouncement.

My grandpa Alfred tried to persuade my parents to let me bring it, and he offered to carry it himself. But my parents would not allow it. I remember the feeling of despair to this day; I can still feel it. I cried, I begged, I cajoled, but the answer was *nein*. And that was it. My red tricycle stayed behind at the train station. Hopefully, someone found it and loved it as much as I did. My parents told me they would get me another one in Prague. Did they know then that would never happen? In some ways, that moment was the beginning of the end of my childhood. Of course, I did not realize it at the time. I didn't understand why we had to go to Prague. I didn't understand why we couldn't live in Karlovy Vary anymore.

Prague was totally unfamiliar to me. It was a big city compared to where I came from. It felt strange and inhospitable, and I was very angry and sad. My family and I moved into a small apartment with a kitchen, a living room, and a couple of bedrooms. We didn't have our belongings because the mover my parents paid to bring our things from Karlovy Vary simply never showed up.

So, there we were, five souls in this little place on the third floor on Italska Street, No. 7. It was not far from Václavské Náměstí, one of the main town squares, a wonderful place, which is close to the center of the city. My grandmother Theresie was very sick at that time. She was always in bed and had to be looked after completely. She had her own room, so the rest of us, my mother, father, grandfather, and I, somehow crowded into the two other rooms.

I was too young to understand these things very well, if at all, but I remember a great deal of tension in our apartment. It is so distressing to me now to realize that my parents were worried constantly and must have been so very distraught and fearful. When I try to imagine that today, as an adult, and having raised a family, I cannot imagine the pressure they were under.

•–•–•

I went back to that same apartment a couple of years ago. My son Asher was with me, and Julie too. I wanted to see the apartment again. Asher knocked on the apartment door and a very nice woman answered. She didn't invite us in, but she was friendly enough. We only spoke for a few moments. I wish I could have seen inside, but it must be very strange, I think, to have people knock on your door so many years later, not knowing what they want and not knowing what to say to them.

Sometime soon, Stolpersteine will be placed in the sidewalk in front of Italska No. 7, one for my father and one for my grandfather. If you ever visit Prague, I hope you can go see them.

Stolpersteine is German for "stumbling stones," and they mark the places where Jewish people lived before they were taken away to all sorts of concentration camps where they were murdered, whether in gas chambers, by shooting squads, or by starvation and overwork. You can find Stolpersteine all over Europe and I think that's sad and wonderful, both. Sad that there are so many, but wonderful that these places are marked. Not too long ago I read an article in the newspaper about the idea of having these types of markers in other places, like America, to show where there were slave markets and other terrible things like that. I agree with this, I really do.

·•·

I do have some memories of our time in Prague. I remember one day, I came home from a stroll with my grandpa and saw my father outside on the sidewalk with a lady who was angry and yelling at him. It turns out a pillow had fallen out of our window and almost hit her. My father apologized profusely and tried to calm her down. I didn't understand what was happening. Then my father went back upstairs, clutching the pillow with both hands. He was very angry with my mother. In fact, I had never seen him so upset. It turns out that my mother was airing out the bedding on the windowsills, as she always did, and one pillow had fallen, perhaps because of a strong wind, which can happen. What my mother did not know was that my father and grandfather had hidden a lot of cash inside that specific pillow for safekeeping because the Nazis had confiscated all the bank accounts and transferred the money to the Third Reich. After that, my mother was very careful about our bedding and that pillow did not get an airing on the windowsill ever again!

In Prague, because of the restrictions against the Jews, my father and grandfather could not work. So one of the big problems was earning money to buy food and to pay for the rent, electricity, and water. In this dire situation, my mother and father decided that to earn money, my mother would go back to her old profession as a milliner. She set up a table, a sewing machine, and shelves and created wonderful hats for well-to-do Czech ladies. She taught me how to sew, and I remember sitting next to her on a little stool sewing clothing for my doll.

Of course, my mother cooked for all of us in that apartment. One funny story that was passed down to me is that my mother had to learn how to cook after she got married. She had not done so before. My father used to go to his mother Theresie's house. She was a great cook. He would eat her food because my mother couldn't cook. Finally, one day, my grandma told my father, "Enough! Your wife needs to learn to cook and you will start eating her food!"

The last family photo I have of my parents together with me must have been taken just before the terrible restrictions on the Jews started. It's a picture of my mother, father, and me swimming in the Vltava River, which runs through Prague. My father is wearing one of those funny, old-fashioned bathing suits with a strap over one shoulder. In the photo, I am getting out of the water and my mother is helping me. I am glad I have the photograph because I do not remember that carefree day at all.

•◆•

The real nightmare for the Jews living in Prague and all over the country started in March 1939. Using the main road to Prague, the German army broke the Munich Agreement and took the country over completely. Hitler himself came to Hradčany Castle in Prague, which is the seat of government to this day, and had his photograph taken. He declared that from then on, the Czech part of Czechoslovakia was now the Protectorate of Bohemia and Morava, part of Greater Germany. The Slovak Republic had broken off and become an independent entity aligned with fascist Germany two days earlier. The Nazis began isolating, segregating, ostracizing, and humiliating the Jews that lived in Prague and the rest of the country.

Of course, I did not understand what was happening, but I've learned since about some of the restrictions placed systematically, one by one, on the Jews in Prague and elsewhere. Jews had to sit in different parts of restaurants. Then, they were not allowed to go to restaurants at all. Jews were not allowed to go out of their homes after eight o'clock at night. Jews were not allowed to ride on public transportation except certain trams and then only at the back and then only if there was room. Jews were not allowed to own cameras, typewriters, radios, phones, or bicycles.

Jews also were not allowed to own musical instruments. My grandfather Fritz, who was living in a different part of Prague, had to turn in his viola, which he loved. I have the receipt he was given. He must have brought that receipt with him to Theresienstadt and given it to my mother so she could get the viola back. But, of course, that never happened. The "receipt" was a ruse. There was never any intention of returning any confiscated item.

As time went on, everything got worse and worse. Even as a little kid, I felt uneasy and afraid. I think children can sense things like that.

My grandfather Alfred used to take me to a little park, right around the corner from where we lived on Italska Street. I loved going to the park and especially this park because there were swings and one of them was in the shape of a canoe. I must have been about five years old. I used to run to that swing and climb right into it, and my grandfather would push me. I was, as they say, in seventh heaven!

And then one day, we went there and my grandpa, who was about ten feet behind me, shouted, "*Nein, nein, nein!* You cannot go there!" He took me in his arms and forcefully pulled me out of the swing. *Nein, nein, nein* he kept shouting. I couldn't understand. Had I been a bad boy? Why was I being punished? I was so scared and upset. I remember hitting him with my little fists. Then, as he held me in his strong arms, he said, "Look up there, you see that big sign? You see? Do you know what it says?" I was five years old, I could not read yet. But he told me it said, "*Juden verboten.*" He tried to explain to me, of course, but I simply could not understand. It was at that time that the restrictions were passed that Jews could not go to public places like parks, swimming pools, or even the river for a walk. Jews were not allowed in any public places or facilities, not even public benches.

Finally, every Jew ten years old and older had to wear a yellow star with *Jude* written on it. If you went out of your house, you had to have that star on the left side of your chest. Germans didn't give these out; Jews had to buy them at the post office. Some people sewed them on their clothes, but that meant you had to buy several for each person. But my mother refused and used a safety pin so she could use the star no matter what she wore. It was her personal revolt, I think, against the Nazis. To this day, I am in possession of that yellow star with the safety pin on the back of it.

During this time in Prague, my grandmother Theresie died. I do not remember her death or her funeral, just that she was very ill. To this day, I am not sure what she died from. She must have been something like seventy years old at the time. It was lucky for her that she died before she was sent to Theresienstadt because older people suffered terribly there. I don't think she would have lived long, especially because she was sick.

Many years later, I tried to find her grave in the New Jewish Cemetery in Prague. I had the exact location of her grave written down, but far too much ivy covered the ground. A couple of years ago, Julie and I went together to look again. We discovered that the reason I couldn't find Theresie's grave is that after the war, under the communist regime, the Soviets took Jewish headstones from that cemetery to use for building roads, repaving squares, and other projects like that.

Then and there, Julie and I decided to have a plaque made to remember my grandma Theresie and all my family members who were murdered and do not have graves. It took some doing and several months, but eventually, the memorial plaque was installed on one of the stone walls of the cemetery. Together, we went to Prague to see it. I was filled with so much emotion. Looking at all those names of my family members who were murdered filled me with both sorrow and rage.

•─•─•

In December 1941, two transports of "volunteer" men were sent from Prague to Theresienstadt (or Terezin, in Czech) to prepare the camp for the "resettlement" of the Jews of Czechoslovakia. My father and grandfather were on the second transport. They were promised they would be treated well and that they would be joined by their families soon.

My father and grandfather came to visit me to say goodbye. At that time, I was in the hospital having my tonsils out. My throat hurt so much, and of course, I couldn't talk. They brought me some ice cream, which is a funny word in Czech—*zmrzlina*. I was not able to say anything, but I understood they were going away.

A few days later, my mother and I received orders to go to Theresienstadt too. I remember dragging a heavy suitcase down the stairs at Italska No. 7. We were told to bring our warm clothes and that we could bring fifty kilograms of belongings.

We went to a train station in Prague. It seemed huge to me, like Grand Central Station. Now I know, of course, that it wasn't a very big train station at all. There were hundreds of mothers and kids there. It was December, so it was freezing cold. It was so crowded and everybody tried to stay in the small space they had. I remember people jostling up against each other as they tried to stay calm and warm. Nobody knew what would happen. There was so much fear.

We had packed some food from home, so we ate a little. It was miserable and frightening. My mother was distraught. She was very sharp with me because, I suppose, I complained a lot about the cold and not having anywhere to lie down. I did not understand what was going on, where my father was, or where we were going. Finally, after two days of waiting and suffering at the train station, we boarded a regular passenger train and left for Theresienstadt. I didn't know it then, but I was prisoner number 885. It was December 14, 1941. I was six years old.

•—•—•

I didn't know if I was doing a good job talking to these German students, but I have never seen a group of kids sit that quietly. I didn't have any photographs to show them or anything like that. But I did seem to have their attention and, to my surprise, their interest, and that gave me the confidence to continue and tell them more. I was surprised at some of the details that I could remember from being such a little kid. Some things really stick with you.

Though it was painful to recall many of my memories, I had the feeling that it might be good for all of us, in the end, because in some ways, it helped build a bridge between us, from the past to future generations.

I explained to the students that, unlike them, I don't have memories of birthday parties, favorite teachers, camping trips, or pets from when I was little. My memories are different. I remember saying goodbye to my great-grandmother on a train platform. I remember hunger. And I remember the tumbling girl.

2

SEARCHING FOR HOPE
IN THE DARK

Gidon (age three) with his grandfather, Alfred Löw.

"ACH, DON'T WORRY ABOUT ME, I AM AN OLD WOMAN. I CAN'T even work. What can they do to me?" These were the last words I remember hearing my great-grandmother say.

Ružena, or Rosa Samish, my grandfather Fritz's mother, arrived in Theresienstadt in July 1942, more than six months after my mother and I did. Three months later, she told my mother she was being sent east. My mother took me to the train platform in the camp to say goodbye to her. I can still see my great-grandmother clearly. She was standing a little bit separate from the other old and suffering people. She was dressed up, wearing a hat and a dark dress. I didn't know where she was going on that train.

·–•–·

My mother and I had arrived at Theresienstadt several months earlier, in December 1941. It was winter and freezing cold and late afternoon when we got there. We had to walk something like two or three kilometers from the small village of Bohušovice because the train did not go all the way to Theresienstadt. The train we were put on was not a cattle car but a passenger train. The Nazis didn't want anyone to panic and flee. They needed to keep up appearances that it was a "resettlement" of the Jewish population.

I remember that long, freezing-cold walk very well. I held on to my heavy suitcase and knapsack and tried my best to keep up with my mother, who was dragging two suitcases. We trudged along for what seemed like hours. I could hardly manage my suitcase. My mother, walking ahead of me, looked back from time to time to see if I was still there. After a while, a man walking next to me helped me out by taking my suitcase. I was exhausted. Finally, we saw barbed wire and guards. There was a great deal of confusion and fear, dogs barking as the Nazi guards ordered us to go faster and get in line and do this and that. I was very little and very scared.

My mother and I were put in the Dresden Kaserne, barracks for women and young children. Each room held about ten souls. There were very tall wooden "bunk beds" that went up three or four levels. There were lice in the mattresses and only cold water to wash with. It was very crowded and noisy. I can still remember the smell. For the rest of her life, my mother always wore lots of perfume because she hated how we all smelled in that camp.

Soon after we arrived, one of the women called out to one of the guards, "So when do we see our husbands, our men, our fathers?" and one of the German guards yelled back that if we wanted to see the men, we should go to our windows at six o'clock the next morning and we would see them going out on their way to work. I was so happy. I was going to see my father!

The morning after our arrival, very early, we kids all craned our necks to look out from our third-floor window, which was covered with bars. I think there were six or seven of us kids, maybe some mothers too. Everyone was looking, and I squeezed in, hoping to see my father. The men were being marched along, five across, and there was my father. I yelled out, "Papa, Papa!" But everyone was yelling "Papa," so I tried calling his name. "Arnošt!" But any men who looked up were hit very hard with a rifle butt, so my father could not look up to see me.

I didn't see my grandfather that day. In fact, I never saw him again.

•◆•

The other children of Theresienstadt, ten years old and up, were organized into groups by the Jewish leadership of the camp, mostly leaders from youth organizations. But I was not a part of this because I was too young and I think my mother wanted me close by her.

The reason the youth leaders organized and taught the children was that they and the Jewish elders did not know their own fates, but they thought if the children could learn and have hope, then that was important for the future. They hoped that the children might have a chance to live. So the leaders tried their very best to create an atmosphere of hope, creativity, and even routine. The German guards allowed this because they had a relationship with the Jewish elders that was cooperative on some levels, as long as the slave labor continued and the elders kept a minimum of order and carried out the Nazis' demands to a T.

Not being a part of those activities with the children, I had to look after myself. I was so hungry all the time and I remember searching for ways to pinch food. I quickly learned that if I could work someplace or help do something, maybe there would be a chance to find a piece of bread. So I searched for things to do: work, dig, clean, carry, whatever presented itself so that I might get a little food.

A truck came all the time to deliver bread. So I learned to meet the truck when it came. I knew the truck had to be unloaded, so I and other kids my age would run and ask if we could help. I remember it was really hard. I was a small kid; taking six, seven loaves of bread in my arms and walking from the truck to the storeroom was difficult, but it could be an opportunity to perhaps break a piece of bread off one of the loaves or find some other things in the storage room.

One time, about three or four of us kids were unloading when we saw in the corner of the storeroom two or three barrels, like wooden beer barrels—huge. And we went over there and saw that marmalade had been in them. We found some cardboard and scraped the inside of the barrels and came away with a little bit of something sweet to put on our bread instead of nothing.

One time a big truck pulled into the yard of Dresden and dumped a mountain of potatoes. Some of them were rotten of course, but they were potatoes. Three or four guards surrounded that mound of potatoes, each with a loaded rifle over his shoulder so that nobody would come close. But, you see, the guards didn't stand only in one place. Each guard had to march stiffly from point A to point B, turn around, and walk back to point A. So, me and two or three other little kids, late in the evening, took little suitcases, very cheap, very light, but easily moved and totally empty. We watched how the soldiers marched from one point to another in a straight line. I had time to get close to the potatoes before the soldier would see me. As he marched from point A to point B, when he was halfway there, that left that space open for me to run to the mound of potatoes, grab a few, and run back before he turned around and could see me. All of us managed to steal a few potatoes; we called this *schleichen*, or what the British call "pinching," stealing. We knew that if they caught us, they would shoot or maybe they would take a whole bunch of kids and shoot us as revenge. But we were so hungry. Everybody was hungry all the time. So we did it and they didn't catch me or the others.

I also managed to find work for a while, for some of the German officers, helping to take care of their horses. A number of us kids learned to go to the stalls every week at a certain time. They would tell us, "Yes, you clean my horse and take care of its feeding and brushing." Sometimes we got a piece of bread or maybe even half an apple. Those of us who did a good job, anyway, which I did! Some of the other kids who didn't do a good job were kicked and slapped, but I was lucky.

I do have to say that it wasn't always dreary and depressing in Theresienstadt. We had a central yard in the Dresden barracks. Not all the barracks had this. We kids wanted to play soccer, but we didn't have a ball. So we took pieces of our old clothing and tore them into strips. We rolled them into a ball and somehow played for twenty or thirty minutes until it fell apart. And that was the end of the game. But I loved it.

I can tell you something quite amazing about me and soccer that I recently learned. In Israel, there is a place called the Beit Theresienstadt Museum. It was founded by survivors of Theresienstadt and is a wonderful educational center. At Beit Theresienstadt, they do many things, including hosting activities that those survivors like me who are still alive can participate in. They also have a great deal of archival information about the camp. One day, they called Julie and they told her that they found a drawing of a soccer game that had my signature on it! So Julie was very sneaky and she asked me to sign my name on a piece of paper. I didn't know what she was talking about. But I did it, and then she showed me the signature and the drawing. It was the same. So, yes, I made this drawing of a soccer game, though I do not remember doing it. It looks like

I used a pencil of some sort and drew a football pitch. And then I drew some funny-looking people playing. I think one is the goalie.

I was overwhelmed by this discovery. But I also had mixed feelings. I felt bad that I didn't remember drawing it, but I felt satisfaction because here was proof, in black and white, that I was there and I was even a little bit creative at the age of nine!

•-•-•

Before the war, in Czechoslovakia, there were a lot of Jewish artists of all kinds. For the Nazis, it was important to say to the world, "Look, all these famous Czech artists and musicians, they're fine. Look, they're playing and performing, and we encourage them to!" So the artists were sent to Theresienstadt.

The Nazis gave the performers a special status in the camp because the Nazis liked to hear them perform. A person today might say, "Oh, Theresienstadt wasn't such a bad place, you had an orchestra." Well, the Nazis decided on the Final Solution for all the Jews at the Wannsee Conference in January 1942. So even in the earliest days of Theresienstadt, the Nazis knew what they were going to do to all of us when the time came. It was all a farce.

The performers and artists at Theresienstadt were not aware that, even as they created, played, and performed, they were doomed. The Nazis wound up transporting most of them to Auschwitz, where they were murdered.

•-•-•

In the first few weeks I was at Theresienstadt, a number of people were executed to make the prisoners understand who was in charge and what the consequences were for anyone breaking the Nazi rules and restrictions. Everybody was told to report to the main square. They'd put up a wooden scaffold, and a Nazi officer said, "You see these men, they sent private letters to their families and friends. This is strictly forbidden and now they are going to pay the price." They brought out several young men and put nooses around their necks. Just as they were hanged, my mother pushed my head to the side so I wouldn't see how they died. The people standing around me were horrified, but they had to stand still and be silent. I remember hearing people gasping. There were shootings too, but that took place at the Small Fortress, not in Theresienstadt itself.

You see, Theresienstadt had two parts: the barracks and the village, which were "repurposed" as a prison for us Jews, and an old prison, the Small Fortress. The fortress was close to Theresienstadt, maybe a half kilometer away. The ARBEIT MACHT FREI sign that you see in pictures hung over the gates to the Small Fortress. Some Jews were there but mainly political prisoners and others, who were kept in horrifying conditions, tortured, shot, and hung regularly.

•◆•

It's important to understand that everybody who survived the Holocaust had their own unique story and experience. For example, I read Ariana Neumann's wonderful book *When Time Stopped*, which is about her grandparents being in Theresienstadt. They had a very different situation than what my mother and I experienced. Arianna's family were able to correspond with people outside the camp, and they even received food and packages. So, some people were allowed some things when other people were not; it all depended on the period of time and the situation. I think this is why some people say that people are lying about the Holocaust, because some stories have differences that seem to contradict.

But the Nazis were full of lies and contradictions, just like how they sometimes used passenger trains or let the artists perform. My mother and I never received letters or packages. There was so much corruption, coercion, and favoritism. You were never sure what would happen next. Some people had slightly better conditions and other people had much worse conditions, and that could change overnight. And, of course, so much depended on the SS commandant; officers in the post changed periodically.

Not just Theresienstadt but other camps, as well, went through different stages according to what was happening in the war and different positions in the camp. The Germans moved people around from camp to camp. It was totally illogical, and it created a pressure cooker in the camp because everybody was always on edge. Theresienstadt started off as a "resettlement" place, but it was really a transport hub and then, by the end, it declined into terrible starvation and disease. Toward the end of the war, they started bringing sick prisoners from lots of other camps and dumping them in Theresienstadt. I remember seeing the bodies lying in the street. I remember the smell. And I remember seeing people who were barely alive, with bulging eyes and bodies that were skin and bones. It was horrible to witness. I tried not to look.

One incident I still don't understand. It must have been in 1944, so I was nine years old. They marched thousands of us from the camp out a few kilometers into a large field. At the edge of the field was a big underground cavern of some sort. A man-made cavern, like an underground parking lot. And we didn't understand what we were doing there. Then they made us all go inside. I think they said this was for us to learn how to hide from bombs or some such reasonable excuse like that. Not that we believed anything they said. I don't remember how long we were there, but we returned to Theresienstadt, and to this day I don't know why they did that. I never saw that place again. There were rumors after the war that they were going to build gas chambers at Theresienstadt too.

My mother remembered many times that we were all marched out into the cold to stand very still to be counted. She wrote about this in the testimonial she gave to Yad Vashem. She said that the children cried from the cold and got beaten and there was nothing the mothers could do about it. I do not remember this.

·-•-·

Because they couldn't work and be useful to the Nazis, the elderly people in Theresienstadt were given many fewer calories than the others, and they quickly became very weak. They put them on the highest floor in their barracks so it was not always possible for the older people to line up for food or go outside.

Some of the other prisoners organized young people to go to the elderly floor and help them.

The conditions for elderly prisoners were cruel and unsanitary. At my age now, I cannot imagine what that must have been like. I need to take my medication each day and be sure to eat enough and see the doctor. My grandfather and the other elderly prisoners had none of those things. I can hardly stand to think about how my grandpa must have suffered so terribly.

Many years later, I saw his death certificate. It said that my grandpa had a "twisted stomach." I cannot imagine what that means, but it sounds horrible. Then, something else broke my heart. The date of my grandfather's death was a year and a half after he arrived at Theresienstadt. I never saw him once during that time. This is truly painful for me to this day. He was such a kindly man and we loved each other so.

.•.

One of my strongest memories from those years is hunger. I was hungry morning, noon, and night. Usually, we were given two meals a day. We had to bring a small tin bowl to get our food. "Dinner" was usually watery soup, a slice of black bread, and sometimes a small piece of margarine. We had potatoes and sometimes they were rotten. I don't remember ever eating meat, except maybe something you might call "meat," and only a very small piece in the bottom of the soup if you got lucky. There was no fruit whatsoever, which probably explains why I can't get enough fruit these days! I don't recall even once having milk or cheese. Sometimes I think that my smaller size to this day might be because I didn't get proper nutrition for such a long period of time. Later in my life, I had a lot of problems with my teeth and my health.

The prisoners at Theresienstadt were used as slaves to make war materials and do all sorts of labor for the Nazis. This is why the Nazis bothered to feed the laborers at all, to keep them alive so they could work.

My mother had to sweep the streets for a while, and then for a short time, she worked in the kitchen. That was a very good job because it meant she could sometimes steal a little extra food for me. Once, my mother pulled a handful of small black golf balls out of her pocket and handed them to me. They were dumplings and probably already rotten, but I ate them anyway and I was thankful!

At one point, my mother and I shared a room with another mother and her daughter, who was about my age. It was a small room, like a walk-in closet, but it was only the four of us, so it felt like a mansion. Early every morning, our mothers were marched out of the Dresden barracks to go to work at the mica factory.

While our mothers worked, the little girl and I stayed behind. We played all sorts of silly games and did tumbling and acrobatics in our tiny room. She was a tremendously agile tumbler. She knew how to do somersaults and stand on her hands and cartwheels and all kinds of things. There was something very special about her.

While we kids looked for food and did our tumbling and tried to stay out of trouble, the women working at the mica factory sat at tables with a small, very sharp knife and had to split mica into very thin layers. The mica, which was called "glimmer" in German, came from a mine in the nearby town of Litoměřice. It had to be split thinly and was used as insulating material in electronics. The Nazis had something they called *schtikprobe*, which means a sample inspection. They would weigh how much mica each woman had split each week, and if anyone was not doing enough, she and her children were sent east. We didn't know it, but those "sent east" were mostly going to Auschwitz. I guess my mother must have worked very hard because this never happened.

Jewish elders in the camp were forced to decide who went on the transport lists. The Nazis would say, "We want five thousand people sent east. You figure out who they are." The Nazis forced the Jews to make terrible choices; this was another way of humiliating and traumatizing every single prisoner in the camp. The people in Theresienstadt tried to get off the list if they could. But the Nazis had requirements of exactly how many people had to be on a transport, so if one person got off the list, someone else was put on.

Sick people were useless to the Reich but still had to be given food, which the Nazis considered a waste. From time to time, the Germans were given orders to empty the sickbeds in the infirmary and send the people east. At one time, my mother developed a serious abscess above her left breast. One of the doctors working in the camp infirmary happened to be our family doctor from Karlovy Vary, Dr. Fischer. He was actually my birth doctor. My mother appeared on one of the lists, and Dr. Fischer managed to remove her name. If she had been sent east, I surely would have been sent with her.

There was a lot of fear of being sent east. I cannot find the right words to express the level of fear, hunger, stress, confusion, and trauma that this caused the people in Theresienstadt. We had no idea what would happen next. But when those transports left, the people on them knew where they were going would be worse than where they had been. I didn't realize it then, but the trains were terrible. People would sometimes spend hours or days on the trains without food, without water, without any sanitary facilities. By the time they finally arrived at their destination, some had died or were close to it.

•◆•

The little tumbling girl and I became best friends. If one can say about a seven- or eight-year-old boy that he can fall in love, then, yes, I fell in love!

It was very cold in the wintertime, and we could never keep warm enough because we didn't have proper clothing or bedding and I suppose we were also far too thin. There were little iron stoves in the rooms to keep us a bit warmer at night. So the little girl and I would go out and collect wood all over the barracks—wherever we could find anything that would burn—sticks, pieces of wood, anything at all. We made an adventure out of it. But one time, we put too much wood in the stove and it became red hot. We were plenty warm enough and very pleased with ourselves, but it was a bit frightening too! Thank goodness, by the time our mothers came back to the room, it had calmed down.

One day her mother came home and told us that tomorrow morning she and her daughter had to report to the train station. The next morning my little friend and I hugged and kissed. I was so sad—tears streamed down my face. Then her mom took their suitcase and they went down to the station. I guess it hurt so much because it was the first time in my life that I felt such a caring, loving feeling for another human being outside of my family. I was completely heartbroken. I lost my friend, my love. Of course, we never heard from them again. They were sent east.

•—•

In January 2024, for the first time, I visited Auschwitz-Birkenau. It was so bitterly cold there, and so barren and so sad. I tried to imagine what it must have been like to endure that kind of cold, cruelty, and misery without proper clothing and being so terribly hungry and frightened. I cannot describe my feelings when I saw the barracks, one after the other, and the crematoria. Finally, so many years later, I saw what being "sent east" really meant.

So many feelings and memories came flooding back to me, of how my special little friend and I played together and the adventures we had gathering wood and trying to stay warm. I thought about how she loved to laugh and play and how much that means to me, even today.

I wanted to say some words for her, in remembrance, but try as I might, I couldn't remember her name. Then I recalled a Jewish proverb that says we die twice, once when we die physically and our spirit leaves our body, and again when nobody says our name anymore. So I decided then and there to call my little tumbling girl Anuška so that we all will remember her for a long time.

3
GATHERING UP THE PIECES

Gidon and Doris in Brooklyn 1949.

I T WAS MAY 8, 1945, AND WE COULD HEAR SHOTS FIRED OUTSIDE.
Then a Russian shell hit part of Theresienstadt. We prisoners did not know it, but we were in the middle of a war zone between the Russians and the retreating Nazis.

We heard shouts from the other side of the barracks. "The Americans are coming!" Somebody else yelled, "It's the British!" Then—"No, Ruskie, Ruskie!" Everybody ran and looked out of their windows. On the other side of the wall with barbed wire all over it, as far as the eye could see, rumbled a long line of tanks and trucks bursting with Russian soldiers with big red flags. We were ecstatic and thrilled! I cannot describe the feeling, even to this day. Some people tore down the fences. Some jumped on the trucks and the tanks. A few people were injured. The soldiers threw candy and cigarettes. Everybody went crazy. My mother was afraid for me to go outside and join the celebrations, but I did it anyway.

Theresienstadt was liberated.

A few months earlier, we kids had seen huge formations of bombers flying over, way up high. They were going to bomb the hell out of German cities. I didn't know until much later the terrible cost of civilian life. But at that time, we knew that something was happening and that the war's end had to be near. We kids shouted and waved at the bombers, even though they could not possibly have seen us. When the Nazi guards saw us, they fired their guns into the air to scare us. We ran, but we were ecstatic. It signaled, we hoped, an end to our suffering.

A few days before the Russians arrived, we'd noticed that things were changing. There were fewer and fewer German Nazis. They had been leaving the camp in droves. There was less food and even less order. Typhoid, a terrible sickness spread through contaminated water and food, was everywhere. In April, thousands of survivors from other camps were sent to Theresienstadt. They were very sick, just skin and bones. There was not enough room for them, and when they died, their bodies were put out onto the street. I didn't go close to them because it was terrible and dangerous. In fact, nobody was allowed to go within a hundred meters of those bodies. The whole camp was put under strict quarantine.

As the Red Army was arriving on the outer perimeter of the camp, they encountered a few of the last trucks of Germans trying to flee. The Russians stopped a truck, took the people out, and marched them into the woods. Then I heard gunshots. I was not shocked, nor did I feel sorry for them. They had caused us such misery for so long. That was my thinking at the time.

There was a Ukrainian cavalry unit too, and they had tired but spirited horses. The soldiers set the horses free and they nibbled at what little grass there was in Theresienstadt. Some of us kids got a hold of them and rode them bareback! It was our first taste of freedom. Then the soldiers set up tents and some sort of field kitchen and began feeding us. For the first time in a long time, we had real food—thick soup with vegetables *and* meat.

The Red Cross came almost right away, along with Czech volunteers from the nearby villages and towns. It was heartwarming to all of us that so many Czechs came to help. So, things started to get organized, and the sick were cared for. There was almost delirious excitement and euphoria; there was also, of course, a lot of anxiety. Where would we go? When were our families coming back? What would be next for us? Would we be able to have normal lives again?

•◆•

A lot of people, when I talk to them about the Holocaust, think that when the war ended and we were liberated, that was the end of the story. But so much had been destroyed for all of us and we had to find ways to start over.

37

After about two weeks, fifteen or twenty of us kids were taken by truck to an abandoned estate nearby. I don't know exactly where it was, but as I recall, the Nazis had used it for officers. There, nurses and volunteers set up cots for us, with clean sheets. They bathed us, even with soap, and they fed us. For me and the others, it was like heaven on earth. But even there, we were not safe.

They let us kids go outside to play. But they warned us to be very careful. As the Nazis retreated, they tried to disappear and mingle with the population. Some of them had done horrendous things not just to Jews but also to Czechs and others. So, as they fled, they threw away their uniforms and sometimes their rifles, too, and their hand grenades. It was dangerous out there in the woods.

One night, I heard kids crying out and I didn't know why. This happened on a number of occasions. It turned out that one of the older kids there was sexually molesting some of the younger kids. Luckily, he didn't get to me, but it was scary and very confusing because I knew it was wrong even though I didn't understand it. I didn't talk about it for a very long time. Though it is a difficult subject, I think it's important to talk about these things today because sexual crimes and violence are another horrible part of war and its aftermath. I did learn much later in my life of many things like this and worse that occurred during the Second World War. I was very lucky that I was not a victim of that kid, but other kids were not so lucky, and for their sake, I felt I should share that this did happen.

After my time in the recuperation center was over, somehow, my mother and I wound up together in Prague. We were very lucky that we didn't have to go to a DP (displaced persons) camp. A lot of people did, and these were not pleasant places to be. Some of them even existed for years, like ersatz villages. They were all over the place.

I don't have clear memories of this time, but I believe we were in Prague for a couple of months at least. My mother was waiting to hear if anyone from our family would come back.

Every morning, I used to get down on my knees near my bed. I prayed to God to bring my father back. Then, one day, my mother saw me and she ridiculed me. She said that my father was not coming back and that it was useless and silly for me to pray. I was humiliated and I was angry with her. Later, she told me that she had spoken to someone who said that my father had died on a death march somewhere near Auschwitz. When my mother told me this, I felt so sad but also very angry. I never prayed again. How could I pray to a God who allowed my father to die like that?

It took many more years until I found out more about what happened to my dad.

·•·

After the war, my mother fed me as much as possible; I was very thin and she wanted me to gain weight. But she was not at all supportive of my mental or emotional well-being. Of course, I was too young to understand her emotional state at that time. She had lost her mother, father, husband, and grandparents. She lost aunts, uncles, and cousins. With only two exceptions that I know of, my mother lost her entire family.

When it became clear that nobody—absolutely no one—was coming back, my mother decided to return to Karlovy Vary. Winding up back in Karlovy Vary was the beginning of a new life for me and for my mother too. I could eat all I wanted and was never hungry. I could rest in a clean bed and sleep without fear for the first time in years. Our home was not far from the central part of Karlovy Vary, so I could walk there easily down the steep hill. A cable train even went right up to the hot spring geyser.

My mother arranged for us to stay in a house with another family that had survived, the Bergmans. It was a small house called the Zentner Hoff. A small courtyard had been used for horses and small wagons long before the war. It is still there today, though the horses are gone. Michael Bergman was a little older than me, and he, too, had survived Theresienstadt, though I did not know him in the camp. We became fast friends.

One day, my mother took a Czech policeman with her and paid a visit to the mover who never brought our belongings to Prague in 1938. Now here was my mother, seven, eight years later, standing on his doorstep with a policeman. She wanted our things back right then and there. Lo and behold, everything—our furniture, pots and pans, porcelain, bedding, my grandma Liesel's Persian rug—was there and being used by the mover. He also had an entire box of our family photos and even my soft-boiled-egg cup that I so loved! We will never know why the mover didn't deliver our things to us in Prague and why he kept them throughout the war. I am not sure whether he was a crook or an angel.

These old, well-worn photos are priceless to me. They are evidence of the past existence of my family, and I treasure them to this very day. One photo is of my grandfather Fritz when he was about three years old. He was born in 1886, so that means this photo is over one hundred and thirty years old. It is amazing to me that I have that photograph today.

.•.

Even though my father and family were gone, I felt at home in Karlovy Vary. But now it was different because it was full of Soviet soldiers and their officers. They were everywhere in my beautiful spa town! They took over the wonderful, big hotels, like the Hotel Imperial, which had tennis courts and gave the soldiers and especially the commanders and generals the nicest, biggest rooms and suites.

I remember that these boisterous young Soviet soldiers roamed the streets and were very full of themselves. After all, they had just vanquished the Nazi army, not a small deed! They loved watches, and if you were a German walking by, especially a young one, they would surround you and say, "Show me your watch!" and then they would take it. Some of these soldiers had three or four watches on their arms from doing this. I got the impression that some of these soldiers, who were only seven or eight years older than me, were a bit drunk, literally so, and also drunk with power.

I was, for the first time in my life, enrolled in school. The school was right around the corner from where we lived. It was September 1945. Luckily, somehow, I could read and write Czech, but because I had never gone to school before, they put me in grade three. I should have been in grade five, because I was ten years old, but grade three was good enough for me. I liked school. I was happy to be learning, although I was behind the other kids in many ways.

I was a small kid in comparison to the others, but I was fast and I was strong!

One day, I was sitting in my classroom and the teacher told us he had to step out for a minute. Maybe for a cigarette. Something like that. Immediately, the kids got up and started going here, there, and everywhere. I stayed in my place. But one of the kids came over to me. I don't know why. He was the bully of the class, a head taller than me. He stood over me and yelled, "*blby Žid!*" That means "stupid Jew." I jumped right up, took my fist, and punched him straight in his nose with all my strength. And guess what? There he was, bleeding. He ran to the corner of the classroom where there was a sink and a faucet for washing up. He tried to wash the blood from his nose. At that very moment, the teacher returned and everybody rushed back to their seats. Then the teacher saw this kid. I think his name was Jiržy. The teacher asked me what happened and I said that I gave Jiržy a box. He asked why and I told him that he called me a "stupid Jew." The whole class was quiet as mice. The teacher told Jiržy to finish washing up and then sit down. And that was that. Nobody ever called me a "stupid Jew" again. It was a thrilling victory, but I must admit, inside I was shaking.

Life took on an almost surreal calm. My mother's cousin John was serving in the US Army stationed in Germany, so he came to see us. It was so wonderful. I even have some pictures of that visit, with me wearing his army cap. John's parents, my great aunt Dora and great uncle Gustav, sent him to the United States in 1937 for fear of what was going on in Germany at the time. For years, John thought that he had been sent away because he had disappointed his parents or done something wrong. Both of his parents were murdered in 1943.

●—●—

A lot of people were trying to find each other using all kinds of agencies and services. Can you imagine what that time must have been like for people? Today we can be in touch with someone almost instantaneously by texting or calling. I can call any one of my kids today just to say hello. But at that time, we didn't have this, we couldn't do a Google search or anything like that. So people didn't know what had happened to their friends and families, sometimes for years.

But somehow, my mother and I were found by my mother's great aunt Flora, who was about eighty and living in Brooklyn with her cousin Leonie and Leonie's teenaged son, Ted. To this day, I do not know how they found us, or how long it took, but once they did, they started sending us packages every month. They were big packages, wrapped in some kind of special cloth. Inside, we found M&M candies, tins of sardines, Spam (which we had never eaten before), and lots of other good things. Every month these packages came, and it was great because there were shortages of just about everything in Europe.

My mother applied for an affidavit, with Flora as our sponsor in America. At that time, there were quotas, even for

Jewish survivors, to immigrate to the United States. In other words, there was a very long waiting list. Also, the Communist Party, with the backing of the Soviet Union, totally took over Czechoslovakia, and getting out became harder. There was a huge amount of uncertainty for everybody about what the future would be like.

During this time, as we waited to emigrate to America, I continued at school and eventually joined a Jewish youth group called Dror, which means "freedom." It had been founded in 1915 in Russia. After the war, a few of those who survived got themselves together and organized and found the older kids and young adults who had also survived the war. In our youth group, we had Friday night gatherings for Shabbat, and we learned many songs and folk dances. We also went camping and hiking and we learned about our history as Jews. It was all very secular, and I fit right in. In fact, I made new friends and I absolutely loved all the activities. To me, it felt like a real home away from home, and for the first time in my life I was proud to be a Jew.

I had heard about people who wanted to become Nazi hunters, to find the Nazis who had escaped after the war and get revenge. And for a short time, I wanted to do this too. I wanted to go after those responsible for what happened to my father and to my family. But I realized that if I did that, I would not be able to build the life that I wanted, with all the things that I had missed out on—a family, friends, freedom, challenges, and adventures.

Many members of the Dror youth group wanted to be a part of establishing and living in a state for the Jews in Palestine.

To me, the idea of us Jews having our own country seemed right and just, after everything we had been through. On top of that, the idea of living and working on a kibbutz, working hard, farming the land, and living in a cooperative community surrounded by nature sounded wonderful. I was bit by the bug.

But my mother wanted to join her cousins in Brooklyn, New York. We simply had to wait to get permission to travel. I had no choice but to stick with my mother and wait until I could make my own choices.

Finally, one day, my mother got a call from the American Consulate in Prague asking us to come in. And, yes, they had good news for us. Two months later, we were on a train to Paris to see Trudé, my mother's cousin. From there, we were to go to the big port in Le Havre. On June 7, 1948, we boarded the SS *America* and sailed to New York. It was such a beautiful ship, "the queen of the American lines." It even had a swimming pool, where they gave swimming lessons. My mother was afraid of water and she didn't want me to take these lessons, but I managed to sneak out and take them anyway. I wanted to know how to swim. My mother and I had our own little cabin, and there was an abundance of wonderful food.

I was so excited to finally see America. Everybody was talking about the amazing Statue of Liberty at the entrance to New York Harbor. I was excited to see it, but it was much smaller than I had imagined. Maybe because we saw it at a distance.

Little did I know that there were such wonders lying ahead on the streets of Brooklyn. At that time, Brooklyn was the center of the Jewish population in New York. Everything and everyone there were Jewish (or so it seemed to me), including the shoe-shine boy, the delicatessen, the dry cleaner, the ice cream shop, the market. I was flabbergasted. It was almost like a Jewish shtetl, but much bigger. I watched the ice cream trucks going down the street and saw places with big glass windows that sold hamburgers and other food. Kids playing stickball, which was something totally new to me. It was all like a dream.

I even started going to the movies. You could buy a ticket at noon, see the movie, and stay and see it again and again. I went by myself. I saw *Batman* and other movies like that and I was totally confused. How could people see through buildings and fly? What a strange country this was. I went home to Leonie, and I asked her in German, "*Was ist das*?!" She tried to explain that it was only make-believe, and her son, Ted, laughed good-naturedly.

It was exciting but at the same time very strange, stressful, and difficult for me because I could not yet speak English and I had no friends. The only people I could speak to were my mother, Leonie, Flora, and Ted, but they weren't my age. I was lonely and a bit lost. But I was also adventurous, so I decided to find friends.

It was June and school was out for the summer, but I enrolled in night school at Erasmus High School to learn English. Not too long ago, I learned that Barbra Streisand also went to Erasmus High School. I love her music and would love to meet her one day.

So, here I was, thirteen years old and the only kid in a class of adults! I did not make friends there because everybody else was older than me. But I did study hard and learned some basic English very quickly. I love languages and today I speak four: German, Hebrew, English, and (still) some Czech and Yiddish. I guess that's three and a half.

Almost every day during that long summer, I went to Prospect Park, which was not far from where we lived. It's such a big park, with a huge pond, trees, playgrounds, and green fields. There, kids played all kinds of games that I had never seen before. They played baseball with a leather glove and a stick to hit the ball. Other kids threw a ball that was shaped like a pregnant banana. It was all very strange for me! Then, one day I saw about a dozen kids my age and a bit older playing a game that I knew—my beloved football. What Americans call soccer. So I watched them play. And every time they missed the goal, I would quickly run and kick the ball back. I did that for about half an hour, thinking that maybe they would ask me to play. And they did! It was hard to communicate with these kids because I was still lacking in English, but I learned that they were part of a Jewish youth group. They invited me to their clubhouse on Friday for Shabbat. They said there would be singing and dancing. I was happy to have found them.

I don't think they knew I was a Holocaust survivor. They didn't ask and I didn't tell them. They knew I was from Europe, so they must have made some assumptions about me. Even then, I didn't want to talk about the past. I simply wanted to make friends. That is the moment when the rest of my life after the Holocaust really began.

4

PUTTING THE PAST BEHIND ME

Gidon's mother, Doris; his father, Ernst; and Gidon in the Vltava River in Prague. Circa 1938.

THE NAME MY MOTHER AND FATHER GAVE ME WHEN I WAS BORN was not Gidon. It was Petr. In fact, my full name was Petr Wolfgang Löw. Not a very Jewish name, I admit! My mother told me that my middle name was Wolfgang because her father, Fritz Samish, who played the viola, loved Wolfgang Amadeus Mozart.

Later, just before I moved to Israel, I changed my family name to Lev, which is a Hebraization of my European family name Löw. For my first name, I chose the name of a warrior in the Bible—Gideon. In Hebrew, this name is spelled גדעון and is pronounced "gid-on," in case you were wondering.

Changing our names was the custom at the time for us Jews who went to Israel. We wanted to distance ourselves from the names we had in Europe, which signified so much pain and suffering. We wanted to put the past behind us.

•—•—

My mother, Doris Samishova Löwova Kohn, was only a little bit older than I am now when she passed away at the age of ninety-two. Our relationship was a complicated and at times painful one for most of my life.

The fact is, my mother saved my life many times while we were in Theresienstadt, and I am very grateful for that. But she was unable to encourage my adventurous spirit after liberation. After the war, I felt that my mother depressed, suppressed, and oppressed me. I wish I had been able, over the years, to break through her anger, depression, and wall of silence. It makes me sad that this never happened. This is one of my few regrets.

I do have very fond memories of my mother in Prague, singing while she sewed her hats. She had a lovely voice and she especially loved operas.

I was happy for her that she was able to find a new husband after the war and maybe even someone who could be my father, but I was unhappy because it meant I had to be uprooted yet again.

•—•—

Just when I was starting to know my way around Brooklyn, make a couple of friends, and speak English, my mother decided to move to Toronto, Canada. I was crushed. We had only been in Brooklyn for a year and I was just beginning to develop a feeling of belonging.

My mother had plans to marry Julius Kohn, whom our family had known in Karlovy Vary before the war. Jus, as we called him, had received permission to emigrate to Toronto. He was alone since his wife and son had been murdered in Auschwitz. The fact is, when Jus was separated from his wife and son in the selections, he ran after them and was beaten almost to death for it. He managed to survive, but his family did not.

When he returned to Karlovy Vary, Jus made a living buying used bicycles. He repaired, painted, and sold them all around Karlovy Vary and other small towns. He took me under his wing and started teaching me so I could help him.

When I think about it now, it may have been painful for Jus to spend time with me instead of his own son, Kurt, who had been three years older than me, whom he surely must have missed terribly. Or perhaps it was good for him to be like a "dad" to me. Looking back now, I cannot imagine how heartbroken Jus must have been, especially so soon after the war.

I don't recall feeling that Jus replaced my father or was in any way like him. To be honest, because I had been separated from my father at the age of six, I really did not have a lot of memories of him to compare one to the other. I simply understood that my father was no longer on this earth, and to this day I do feel his absence very deeply.

Of course, I have a few photographs of my father, from before the war. A couple of years ago, someone sent me a photograph of my father that I had never seen before. It really shocked me. This photograph was taken in 1941, shortly before we were all sent to Theresienstadt. Though this photograph was taken only about four years after the last photo I have of us, all three, swimming in the Vltava River, in this photo, my father looks completely different. He looks very tired, worried, and much older than his age. He was applying for a visa to get out of Czechoslovakia. My mother told me that my father did try to get us out of there but that he didn't want to leave his parents behind, Grandpa Alfred and Grandma Theresie.

To me, Jus was a warm family friend, we got along well, and I loved learning the mechanics of bicycles from him. Once, when Jus had taken me with him on our bicycles to buy some butter out in the country, the chain came off my bike and I went crashing down a hill and landed in some bushes. Jus helped me get up, dust myself off, and put the chain back on so we could carry on.

I was aware that Jus and my mother were "seeing" each other and had developed a relationship, but when my mother and I finally got permission to emigrate to the United States, I don't recall that they stayed in touch. I must have been wrong about that because, in 1949, I was uprooted again.

•◆•

Our life together, my mother, Jus, and I, was not a happy one. My mother and Jus had a lot in common, which is probably what brought them together. They had both lost their spouses and families in the war, they were starting over in a totally new country as newcomers, and they both shared a lot of sorrow. They were two very injured human beings. My mother was very depressed and angry, and she argued with Jus and with me too. Once, when she locked Jus out of the house, I felt so badly for him.

Looking back, I regret not ever having thanked Jus for trying to be a father to me. I wish I had. My feelings for Jus were very warm, and years later, when my youngest son, Asher, was born, I gave him the middle name of Julius in memory of Jus. To this day, I have Jus's small leather eyeglass, which he used for stamp collecting.

My mother and I never talked about what happened in the war, and the fact is, my mother never, ever, for the rest of her life spoke to me about her losses and pain. It is one of my very few painful regrets that I did not, in later years, try harder to speak to her and share our memories and feelings together. When I was grown, I did try from time to time, but my mother did not open up. She told me that she tried to see a therapist but that she didn't continue. There are so many things I wish I could ask her about today.

Luckily for me, I attended the Central Technical School and that kept me very busy and got me out of the house. I even tried out for the junior football team! I did three months of training before I could try out for the team. I was fast and agile, but the coach told me I was too light. I was so disappointed. But many years later, I played a lot of tag football with my kids when they were growing up. Our whole family loved it.

The football coach was also my favorite teacher, Wally London. He taught English literature and geography. I will never forget how Mr. London had each one of us, in order to get a passing mark in English, memorize a poem from the curriculum that we had just learned.

I wish I knew why I chose to memorize Antony's speech from *Julius Caesar*, but it has stayed with me. To my amazement, I still can recite the first few lines.

Friends, Romans, countrymen, lend me your ears;
I come to bury Caesar, not praise him.
The evil that men do lives after them;
The good is oft interred with their bones;
So let it be with Caesar.

I think of Mr. London very often. I believe he really cared about his students. He made me feel good and confident.

—•—

I did a lot of odd jobs after school. I wanted to save up to buy myself a Raleigh bicycle. One day, I went on the main street called College Street, which was the center of the Jewish population there in Toronto, and I went from shop to shop and started asking for jobs. Finally, I found a place called Seaman's Fish and Food Store. It was a grocery store where Mr. Seaman also smoked the fish that were delivered to him in boxes filled with ice. Part of my job was to prepare the fish for smoking. I had to descale the fish, cut them open, remove the insides, and then put them on a hook to be smoked. My hands got so cold doing this job!

Besides the fish, I had to keep the shelves full of goods and other products. Mr. Seaman had an old bike and I used it to make deliveries. I usually got a nickel tip, minimum, besides being paid eight dollars a week by Mr. Seaman.

Once, a big shelf fell on me. I wasn't hurt, but Mr. Seaman said he would raise my wages by two dollars a week, so then I was receiving ten dollars a week! I was thrilled and even hoped another shelf would fall on me and I would get another raise, but this didn't happen.

Eventually, I had enough money to buy an English-made bicycle, a blue Raleigh that had a big basket in the front. With such a lovely bicycle, it was much easier to make deliveries. I saved up enough money to buy my mother and Jus a brand-new radio, which they loved!

Later, when I got a bit older, I learned how to drive and I purchased a green Hillman car from Jus for something like $500. This really gave me a feeling of independence.

Once, my mother asked me if I could help get rid of an old Persian carpet that had belonged to her mother. It was one of the things the "mover" had held onto and we got back after the war. I remember this carpet quite well, because we had used it in our living room for some time. It had lost its luster and was a bit worn, but it was lovely, with red, blue, green, and other colors. To me, it was special because it belonged to my grandmother. But my mother said, "Just get rid of it. Maybe you can even sell it." I think she wanted to get rid of painful reminders of the past.

So, I did what she asked me to do. Let me tell you, that carpet was heavy! Together with a friend of mine, we loaded it on the Hillman car roof and went to the closest rug store, unloaded it, and brought it in only to be told that they did not deal in used carpets. So we loaded the rug back onto the car roof and drove to another store and lugged it in again. The man looked, then shook his head and said he would give us $100 for it. By now, my friend and I were both tired, but I was not going to give the carpet away for so little.

So we rolled the carpet up again, loaded it back onto the car roof again, and went to another store. This time the owner looked the carpet over carefully and said it was a genuine Persian carpet but it needed a lot of repairing and cleaning, so he was sorry, but all he could offer was $16,000, take it or leave it. My friend and I looked at the floor, we looked at the wall, we didn't look at each other because we could barely suppress our surprise. But we left with a check that I brought home to my mother and she could not believe it. Neither could I! I wonder who owns it now.

•◆•

Even though I was going to school and had a number of jobs, I was still very involved with my Jewish youth group and dreaming of living in Israel. When I look back, I realize that my youth group became like my family and gave me the encouragement that I did not get at home.

Eventually, I even became a camp counselor and led many hiking and camping trips into the beautiful Canadian wilderness. In my youth group, the whole idea of scouting was to teach the kids to work together, help each other, and cooperate as they solved problems and challenges. We also taught them the skills they would need to enjoy and respect nature, like how to tie different knots, how to pitch a tent, and how to build a fire. I became very good at all these things, as you can imagine.

One such camping trip stands out in my memory. I had taken a group of six or seven boys who were eleven or twelve years old on an overnight hike in the Laurentian Mountains, in Quebec. This must have been about 1954 or 1955.

As we were hiking in the mountains, which were very wild and beautiful, from time to time we would see small, isolated cottages. We were looking for a good place to pitch our tents. We came to a steep drop-off, and when we looked over it, we saw a beautiful green-blue lake. It was so lovely and quiet. We wanted to climb down and go swimming, but we knew we would have to climb back up again, and some of the kids weren't too sure they could do it. But I led the way and, yes, we climbed all the way down and jumped right in that cold water and swam while the fish tickled our feet.

Later on, we dried off in the sun, ate our lunch, climbed back up the steep embankment, and continued on our way. After a while, we came to a large hotel or resort of some kind. It had a big green lawn and a long driveway. It looked like a castle. There were signs here and there, but they were written in French. One of the kids spoke French and he pointed to one sign that said, in no uncertain terms, that Jews were not allowed there. I could not believe it. I asked him to read each word and to explain. The sign said DOGS AND JEWS NOT PERMITTED.

I was shocked and very upset. One of the kids said, "Let's go break their windows!" Believe me, I was very tempted to do just that—or at least confront the hotel owners—but I knew it wouldn't do any good. Probably the hotel owners would call the police, and then what would happen to the kids?

Later on, after we pitched our tents and made our fire, I told the kids where and when I had seen that kind of sign before. Of course, they had a lot of questions for me, but I was not eager to tell my story. I didn't want to scare them.

·•·

Finally, in 1959, more than ten years after I had left Europe behind me, I said goodbye to my mother and Jus and boarded a ship in New York Harbor. Once again, I saw the Statue of Liberty, but this time it got smaller and smaller as I sailed toward a new life, thousands of miles away. My dream of living on a kibbutz in Israel was finally coming true.

Of course my mother and Jus were sad to see me go and a bit apprehensive about my new adventure, which they did not understand. But I was determined to build a life of my own. I remember how they stood there on the dock, arm in arm, and waved goodbye, Jus with his mop of blond hair, so much taller than my petite mother.

I was young, only twenty-four years old, and I was prepared to work hard and overcome any challenge that would come my way. I was sailing into my future and away from the past.

5

JUMPING INTO THE
DEEP BLUE SEA

Gidon and Susan circa 1971.

TWENTY-FOUR HOURS AFTER SHE ASKED ME TO MARRY HER, I called Susan Deborah Kashman and said yes. Even up to this day in my life, it was the craziest thing I ever did!

•-•-•

When I arrived in Israel in 1959, I had only a suitcase full of clothes, a stack of 78 rpm records, and a record player. Kibbutz

Hazorea was only about an hour's drive inland from Haifa. I rode in the back of a truck and admired the sights along the way as we bumped down the road—the great, wide valley, the palm trees, the hills, and the flowers. It was like no place I had ever been or could have imagined. Everything was different; the air was different and even the sea was a bluer blue.

Not once during that bumpy ride did I doubt my leap of faith to follow my dream of being a kibbutznik. Somehow, I knew that I could handle whatever was thrown my way.

The other newcomers and I were greeted very warmly at the kibbutz and given a big meal to eat in the dining hall. The food was so fresh and plentiful, with lots of cheeses, bread, butter, fish, chicken, fruits, vegetables, and so on.

There were no dormitories, so for a place to sleep at night, I was given a "lift," which was a sort of large wooden box that had been used as a cargo container for shipping. It stood on cinder blocks, high up on a hill overlooking the Jezreel Valley. It was a wonderful view but also very lonely. At night, little mice would come to visit me, and at times lizards, too, were my companions.

Sixty-two years later, by coincidence, I learned that I had cousins living about thirty miles away from that lonely lift on the hill and I never knew it! They were my mother's cousins who came to Palestine in 1928 and managed to escape Hitler and the Nazi regime.

When I arrived at my kibbutz, a few hundred other kibbutzniks lived there. Everybody was divided into different jobs and roles to keep the kibbutz in good working order. There were orchard workers, kitchen staff, cowshed workers, laundry workers, chicken coop tenders, and many more such duties to take care of every day. The idea of a kibbutz was to be a self-sufficient cooperative community where everybody worked hard and everybody was equal. I loved it.

I had hoped to work in the dairy barn, but instead I was assigned to work in the grain elevators that supplied the various grain mixtures for all the animals on the kibbutz: cows, calves, chickens, and sheep. In this role, I learned how to drive a tractor with a grain delivery bin, back it up carefully, and add exactly the right amount to each grain bin. I learned how to unload and stack hundreds of sacks of grain into sometimes twenty-foot-high stacks. One day, a stack of barley sacks weighing a hundred pounds each came crashing down because I had not stacked them properly. My boss, Rafael, was not too happy with me, but with the true spirit of a kibbutznik, he helped me put everything back in order and I learned a valuable lesson.

Many other people on the kibbutz were becoming couples and I wanted to find someone too, but I did not think of myself as a good-looking guy and I was not very confident with the ladies. But I did know how to dance. I started a weekly folk dance evening at the kibbutz so I could get to know people better and we would enjoy ourselves.

At the very first folk dance lesson, I quickly discovered that my record player wasn't loud enough. So we found an amplifier, connected it, and off we went, dancing in the dining hall, all of us, together.

•-•-•

I met Susan Kashman in 1961. She was visiting Israel for a few months, on a program that allowed young people to learn Hebrew and experience living on a kibbutz. Lots of young people came to Israel to do that, Jewish and non-Jewish alike. Susan worked at the furniture factory on my kibbutz, and the first time I saw her, she was covered with sawdust, from head to toes, from sandpapering the legs of wooden stools. I'll never forget the sight of her. Even covered in dust, Susan was so beautiful to me, with her long, dark hair and shining eyes. A spark of intelligence and warmth emanated from her that drew me to her instantly. I was definitely attracted to her, body and soul.

Susan and I became very good friends, and a while later, when she returned to the United States, we kept in touch. It was my habit to keep in touch with friends, and Susan was the recipient of yearly news cards and holiday cards from me to her. From time to time, she responded with letters and cards. In essence, for the time being, we went our separate ways.

My life on the kibbutz continued, and after a few years, I got married to a pretty redheaded American who had also come to Israel on the same program as Susan. My first wife and I had a ten-year age difference. We came from very different backgrounds and our relationship was very stormy, to say the least, even after—and maybe especially after—we had two little redheaded children, a daughter and a son. In fact, we eventually parted very bitterly and came up with an unusual way of sharing custody of our two children. My firstborn, my daughter Maya, would live in Jerusalem with her mother and her new partner, and our son, Yanai, would live with me on

Kibbutz Zikim. Looking back now, I realize this was a ridiculous arrangement, but we had agreed to it and that's the way it was.

•─•─•

In 1970, Susan's parents, Margie and Monty Kashman, decided to move to Israel. The assassinations of Dr. Martin Luther King and Robert F. Kennedy left them feeling very disillusioned. Sue sent a package for me along with them. Two of the items I had requested, a Tonka truck for my son and a coffee percolator (which we did not have in Israel at that time). Susan also sent two albums: *Bridge over Troubled Water* by Simon & Garfunkel and a Mozart violin concerto, both of which I listened to endlessly and loved. Little did I know that the Simon & Garfunkel record would become the soundtrack of my life together with Susan. For that matter, little did I know I would have a life together with her at all!

I was overjoyed when, finally, Susan returned to Israel after she finished her studies in the United States. She wanted to be closer to her parents. She moved into a small apartment on Allenby Street in Tel Aviv.

By that time, I was living on a different kibbutz, Kibbutz Zikim, which was about an hour south of Tel Aviv. At that stage, there was nothing romantic between us. Sue was in a relationship with a Russian cellist of some renown, but it was, from what she said, a very volatile relationship. I will admit to you, I was a bit jealous.

Because of my painful divorce, I was attending group therapy sessions every week in Tel Aviv. I took a bus there from

Kibbutz Zikim and I always stopped to call Susan before the meeting to find out how she was.

One day, when I called, Susan sounded distraught. She said that I needed to come see her right away. Her exact words were: "Gidon, I need to talk to you, I need you. Please, come." I reminded her that I was going to my therapy session as usual, and she said, "We'll have our own therapy this time! Please come!" I didn't know what was going on, and I was reluctant to miss therapy, but Susan sounded truly desperate, so of course, I went to her.

Shortly after I arrived at Susan's tiny little apartment on Allenby Street, which she shared with a roommate, she told me that her relationship with the cellist was over and done. The sadness, pain, and disillusionment of how she felt all came pouring out. Through her tears, she told me that she was pregnant. I must admit, I was shocked. Here was this woman I had known for ten years and she was in real trouble. It was clear to her, and then to me, that she was determined to keep this baby even though she felt that she wasn't up to raising a child on her own. The cellist had made it equally clear to Susan that he was not prepared to be the father of this child and he was not prepared to marry her. Sue needed help. Of course, she knew about my predicament too, that I was a single parent of a little boy. So, Susan came up with an extraordinary idea.

••••

When Susan asked me to marry her, and to "join our fortunes," my initial reaction was a mixture of disbelief, shock, joy, and a jumble of mixed feelings. Susan Kashman wanted to marry *me*? Wow! After the shock subsided, my feelings and hopes came to the rescue. I asked Susan, who had other male friends, why me? She said, "Gidon, we have known each other for more than ten years and you are the only dependable man I know." I took a deep breath and told her that I needed to think about it.

It was true that the friendship between Susan and me had, once or twice, been a bit romantic, but we had been on different paths and the timing was never right. Now I had a big question to think over.

As I sat on the bus on the way back to Kibbutz Zikim after seeing Susan, my mind was working double time. We were very different in many ways. Susan was American and educated and literary. She had degrees in American history and English literature. She was an only child from a warm family in Brooklyn. She was sensitive and expressive and loved to write poetry. Would Susan be able to be a mother to my wonderful, boisterous, inquisitive little boy? Would I be able to be a father to her unborn child? Could we grow to really love and care for each other as a family? I thought about all this and more.

The next day, I called Susan, and this time, I was the one who asked a question: "So, are you ready to jump with me into the deep blue sea and learn how to swim?"

The wedding took place on one of the sprawling lawns on the kibbutz, with the entire kibbutz membership in attendance. Susan's aunts flew in from America, and her parents, Monty and Margie, were there too, of course. A few of our friends from around the country were also present. My mother and Jus were not able to join us, though they did send us a nice present so we could go on a holiday. Sue wore a wonderful white wedding dress with lovely Yemenite embroidery in the front. She looked lovely in it. You couldn't tell that she was more than five months pregnant. It sure was a time of high excitement for us both! We ate, we drank, we danced and were truly happy.

And yes, very quickly, Susan learned how to be a mother to my son, Yanai, and the day our lovely daughter Hadasa was born, I was so excited to see her that I climbed a tree outside the hospital to try to glimpse Sue and our new daughter. Hadasa was so tiny and perfect, I'll never forget it. I'm lucky I didn't fall out of the tree!

•─•─•

Not too long after our wedding, I was offered a job in Wales to work for a company that manufactured dairy equipment. This company had come to Israel and set up, at my kibbutz and a number of others, a brand-new type of modern milking machine, and I had been trained to use it. Because I spoke English in addition to Hebrew, they wanted me to come to their facility in Wales and work for them.

So, there Sue and I were, having been married for a little over a year and expecting our third child, with a big decision to make. Should we uproot ourselves and go live and work so far from our home? We decided that it was a once-in-a-lifetime chance and said yes. So, we got on a plane and off we went!

We loved it there in Wales. It was totally different from Israel—so green because it rained so often. I used to go to the pub with my workmates even though I don't drink beer. Our son Shaya was born in Wales in January 1974. He was breech, so extra nurses and doctors were present in case it would be a difficult birth. They told me to go off and wait. I hadn't even sat down when a nurse came running. "Mr. Lev! You have a son!"

When I saw Shaya for the first time, he was all wrinkled and looked like an old man. He reminded me of Grandpa Alfred. Today people think Shaya and I look a lot alike and I think that's true.

Eleven months after we arrived in Wales, my work permit expired and we had another decision to make. Should we return to Israel or have ourselves another adventure and try out America for a while? Off to America we went!

For the next few years, Susan and I moved many times as we searched for the right place to live, whether that was in America, Canada, or Israel. By then, we had a pretty big family, which meant a great deal to us both. We had another son, Elisha, who was born in Israel in 1979, and our youngest, Asher, who was born in Canada in 1981. Today my kids and grandkids have many different passports!

•◦•

One of my favorite family adventures is when I took the kids camping all across America. We were living in Canada at that time, and I wanted to see some of America and to go to California to visit with friends. We couldn't afford plane or train tickets, so we had to drive. Sue had gotten a new job at a community center and she couldn't join us. Besides that, I think she really needed a break. I decided to go it on my own with five kids, the youngest only two years old! We would camp our way across America and get to California. Looking back, I'm amazed that I did this and that Susan trusted me to do it.

Before we left, the kids and I spent two weeks practicing putting up a tent in our backyard. Even little Asher, only two years old, was a part of the team, holding the center pole. We got it down to seven minutes. We planned to all sleep in one tent, which we had special ordered.

On the first of August, the kids and I piled into our station wagon and took off. My son Yanai was sixteen, and he sat up front with me as my navigator. In the next row of seats sat Hadasa, eleven, Shaya, nine, and Elisha, four. Asher sat in a car seat way in the back, and let me tell you, he cried every time we buckled him up! Our tent and clothing and other supplies we'd tied on top of the car. I am sure that anyone who saw us must have wondered what we were up to, a dad and five kids.

We sang and played games in the car and stopped for lunch and to see the sights. Sometimes we were the only ones on the road. We had to be careful not to run out of gasoline because there weren't too many filling stations on the way. Whenever possible, we would wade into lakes or streams to swim and wash ourselves.

At one such stop, in the late afternoon, while it was still light, we arrived at a large reservoir where a lot of people were picnicking and swimming. We chose a suitable spot nearby and put up our tent. By the time we had finished, we were the only ones there, so we all undressed and, without bathing suits, jumped into the clear, clean water, all six of us! It was refreshing and energizing, and the kids got nice and clean. Then we started a fire and cooked a really good meal of potatoes that we'd wrapped up and baked in the fire.

I gave Yanai several maps, and together we planned our route every day. We two made it a point to stop before it was dark so we could choose a good camping spot, set up our tent, make a fire, and fix something to eat. And then get the little ones into the tent to sleep.

But once, in Wyoming, we stopped a bit too late because Yanai and I had misjudged the distance and the time it would take us. We ended up arriving after nightfall. It was very dark and the kids were hungry and tired. By the time Yanai and I were done fixing our meal over the fire, the kids had all collapsed in the tent and were fast asleep. Yanai and I had a quiet, calm, and delicious evening meal together, just the two of us. We enjoyed each other's company and looked forward to seeing where we were in the daylight the next day.

When we all woke up the next morning, it was truly amazing. It was like being in the middle of a towering rock forest! I couldn't believe how lucky we had been to find a small clearing for our tent the night before when it was so dark. We were surrounded by big black rock formations. Of course, the kids wanted to climb on the rocks. Even Asher tried. Before too long, once more, we folded the tent, rolled up the sleeping bags, made eggs and tea for breakfast, and set out for another day on the road.

We traveled through Nevada, Montana, Nebraska, Iowa, Utah, and many more places. Our car broke down once, but we got it repaired after a few hours. Another time, we got a flat tire, but someone helped us right away. The kids got along pretty well most of the time, although they argued from time to time. But we did manage to make it all the way across America and all the way back again—one dad with five kids! The kids were exhausted and happy when we returned home. We all felt a great sense of accomplishment and had so many new experiences. I especially felt a sense of accomplishment and joy that I was able to take all five kids on such a long and adventurous trip and that we made a lot of memories and came home in one piece.

•◆•

In 1984, Susan and I decided to return to Israel for good. We didn't have a lot of money, so we rented an apartment. After some time, we did manage to build a humble home on HaGai Street, No. 47, in Nof HaGalil, which is right next to Nazareth. Both towns are up high in the hills, overlooking the Jezreel Valley.

Our home had a nice garden in the front and the back, with orange and lemon trees. I remember how sweet the blossoms smelled in the spring! We used to pick the fruit from the trees. Later on, we added a downstairs apartment where my mother lived eventually. Asher built himself a tree fort there, and he was always busy hammering away, which drove my mother crazy.

I supported my family by becoming a milk tester. The Ministry of Agriculture needed to make sure that the milk that dairy farmers sold was of good quality, free from antibiotics, and healthy for people to drink. Today, testing the milk is done by machine, and the results are sent online. But at that time, these samples had to be collected one by one, from each cow, and each sample had to be identified with the cow's number and registration.

With five kids at home, being a milk tester was a good way of life for us because I had to work only ten days per month and the rest of the time I could help Sue with the kids and take care of our home. But what a ten days! I had to take samples of milk from three thousand cows on about twenty farms! Susan and I talked about how we could meet this challenge, and we came up with an idea. We would do it as a family. Our children would learn to respect hard work and have the feeling of satisfaction that they were helping out.

At first, some of the farmers, seeing me and my kids get out of the car, were a bit skeptical. Asher was so young, but there he was with a notebook, pencil, clipboard, and the small sample bottles, and the farmers would say, "What is he doing here?" But the kids did a good job and the farmers came to like and even respect them.

We always stopped in Nazareth on the way home and went into one of the falafel shops, where each one of us chose what to put into our falafel, like hummus, tahini, cucumbers, and tomatoes, and of course the delicious falafel balls themselves, all wrapped in fresh pita bread. Sometimes we would even ask for some chips to top it off. I still love chips like that, made with fresh potatoes in lots of hot oil and salt.

Our family loved having adventures. I guess the apple doesn't fall too far from the tree! We camped, we hiked, we lived in different homes in different countries, but always, we had each other. All the kids turned out to be hardworking, intelligent, and creative. A lot of that is due to Susan and her wonderful, creative, expressive spirit.

•–•

The last photographs our family took together were taken beneath our beloved purple jacaranda tree in front of our home in Nof HaGalil. Our son Elisha, who is a talented photographer, took photos of each of us under that tree, with the petals falling all around us. At that time, Susan was so weak she was in a wheelchair.

Susan took her last breath exactly as she wished to. She was at home, in her bed, surrounded by all of us. It was June 2012. When the final moment came, it was one of the most difficult moments in my life. Susan shook and struggled, and I held her hand and squeezed it for the last time. Then my dear Susan was gone.

•–•

At the wedding of our son Elisha to his beautiful bride, Eti, Susan didn't feel good, she didn't have any energy. She had been feeling that way for at least a week already. So we took ourselves to the doctor. The doctor thought Susan had pneumonia, so he took some X-rays and put her on antibiotics right away.

Not long after that, we learned that Paul Simon, of our beloved Simon & Garfunkel, was coming to Tel Aviv to play a concert, and the whole family decided we just had to go and see him perform. We all helped organize how we would get there, from the train station to the stadium. We had to walk some distance from the train station, and it was very hard for Sue. She was very weak. But we went, and we all loved the concert so much. We knew almost every word to every song, and to our surprise, so did everybody else! We thought that Simon & Garfunkel was our special family secret. The concert lasted three hours and of course Paul Simon played Sue's favorite song, "Slip Slidin' Away."

Not too long after that, we got Sue's diagnosis. I'll never forget that moment. The doctor told us that Susan had lung cancer that had spread in both lungs and that he could not operate.

Susan sat quietly and then looked at me and said, "Please, just don't let me die in a hospital."

I said, "You're not going to die yet! We'll try everything possible!" I was devastated but determined that we would find a way to save Sue and turn this situation around.

There were many doctors, tests, and treatments, some of them experimental. Then we learned that the cancer had metastasized and gone to her brain.

In the last couple of months of her life, our son Asher came home from his travels and sat with Susan every day. Susan told me they talked about absolutely everything—life, poetry, music, love, and much more. It was a very special time for them both. I was not privy to their conversations; it was between mother and son.

It was less than a year after her diagnosis that Sue passed away, at home, in her bed, as she wanted to. We were all absolutely devastated.

Our family sat shiva (the seven days of mourning customary in the Jewish religion), and even though I am not a religious or observant person, I feel that it is a very good tradition. It was very warm and loving. So many people came each day, including many friends of our children, which really touched me. They brought more food than I could ever eat, and everybody had such wonderful stories to share about Susan. You see—even in the sorrow of death, there was something good.

•-•-•

Then I was alone in our beautiful home, which was filled with so many memories of our life together. It was so hard. I didn't know what to do with myself. I was seventy-seven years old, and Susan and I had lived our lives together for forty years. She was the driving force in our home. I felt aimless, lost, and abandoned. My kids were adults and were busy living their own lives, having relationships, building their families, and coping with the day-to-day challenges of life.

I went to the grocery store and cooked simple food like soups and rice. I took care of the endless paperwork required when someone leaves this earth. I went back to work driving a taxi. But I admit, I was heartbroken and very lost.

One day, not too long before Susan died, she had looked at me and said, "Gidon, when I am gone, don't stay alone." I was sitting in our yellow armchair and I started to cry. Then Sue smiled a little bit and said, "I know you. You won't stay alone." That memory still brings me to tears. Susan understood me. She knew that I am not a solitary person.

A few months after her passing, I told a friend that I was lonely. He suggested that I go on a Jewish dating app called JDate. I missed Sue with all my heart, but I wanted to continue living and making the most of what life I had left. I didn't want to stay alone.

It was very strange and I didn't know how to do it, exactly, but I guess the ladies liked my photo because I did receive many messages. I enjoyed this experience of getting to know new people. Somehow, it made me feel as if, yes, my life was continuing. I had short relationships with a couple of girlfriends, but then I met Julie.

I was looking for someone to help me write down the story of my life. I asked around, and someone gave me Julie's name. I called her and told her that I was a Holocaust survivor and that I had written down my story. Julie agreed to meet me for coffee because, it turned out, we lived near each other. When I came into the café to meet her, I came upon this young, pretty, warm, and friendly California woman, and we liked each other immediately. Julie said that she would try to help me out, but she was more enthusiastic about me than the book I wanted to write! In fact, she called me two days later and invited me for coffee again. I was flabbergasted.

Soon, we were seeing each other almost every day. We went to movies and we went grocery shopping together and, yes, we talked about my story. A few months later, we decided to live together.

Some people might think that entering into another relationship after your spouse passes away is somehow wrong, but I do not agree with that. There is a great deal of love that we can give and receive and it does not in any way diminish or devalue the love and life we had with our previous partners. The opposite may be true—it enhances the value of our previous partnerships because they gave us the tools to love again and again and again.

Julie has been good for me in the last chapter of my life. I am lucky that I met her and that she loves me and I love her. I am lucky that she took a chance on this old guy!

·—•—·

I have jumped into the deep blue sea a number of times in my life and had to learn to swim. I have been defeated too, and I have made many mistakes that I had to dig my way out of. But those things made me stronger and more determined. When we overcome adversity, we find out just how strong and creative we really are—and we can surprise ourselves! If we don't try things and take chances, we will never know what we are capable of.

Sometimes people ask me how I have gotten through so many things in my life. I tell them that somewhere, way up in the sky, there must be a lucky star looking over me.

Lucky star or not, the fact is, as far as I can tell, we only have one life, so why not live it to the fullest? I have always asked myself, from an early age until now, "What have I got to lose? What is the worst that could happen?" I like to take chances and push boundaries, especially my own! I simply have an inner belief that if I just keep trying, unexpected and good things might happen—and they often do.

6

BECOMING A VOICE AND A REASON FOR HOPE

Gidon in Dubai 2023.

I's HARD FOR ME TO BELIEVE THAT I BECAME THE FIRST HOLOCAUST survivor to speak in the United Arab Emirates at an official diplomatic event or that I would make videos with Israeli pop stars and even have the opportunity to meet Elon Musk.

For almost fifty years, I did not talk about my story. We, all of us who survived the atrocities of the Nazis, simply had to move forward because it was clear there was no going back.

I don't believe that mental health or trauma was very well understood or dealt with at that time. Being a kid when the war ended, I took my cues from my mother. She had a lot to deal with herself, of course, and was also trying to cope, like everybody else who had come back alive.

When I came to Israel, I don't recall that anyone asked me about what had occurred during those years in Theresienstadt, and I didn't bring it up. I know of a couple Holocaust survivors who came to Israel after the war, and they were not at all understood or treated well.

At that time, Jewish people who'd lived in this area for twenty and more years prior to 1945 were interested in creating what they called "the new Jew," someone who was strong, independent, free, and ready to fight for themselves. So, when the survivors arrived, they looked at them a bit askance and asked, "Why didn't you fight back?" or "How could you let them do this to you?" It wasn't only like that, of course. Many survivors came to Israel after the war and were received and treated warmly. But they were not understood. People in Israel at that time felt that in life you must be strong, work hard, build a country, defend it, and of course create a family because children were our future. Talking about the Holocaust was, in a way, looking backward, not forward. It wasn't encouraged; it wasn't a topic. I was still a long way from thinking about my story, much less talking about it with others.

In 1960, about a year after I arrived, I was called up to serve in the Israeli Defense Forces (IDF). The IDF is a conscription army, so everybody has to serve two or more years. I knew that

I would be called up and I looked forward to the challenge. And a challenge it was! Because of my "advanced" age—I was a few years older than many of my commanders—it was not always easy. I was also small in stature, so some of the physical challenges were tough. But I was determined to do my part, and I did my best. During basic training, I even taught the entire base "Michael Row Your Boat Ashore" as a marching and running song!

Of course, I made new friends in the army, but I often felt lonely. I didn't have any family at all, only my mother and Jus, and they were far away in Canada.

The following year, 1961, Adolf Eichmann was put on public trial in Israel. He had been hiding in Argentina when the Mossad found him. Eichmann was one of the highest-ranking SS officers, responsible for coordinating the transport of millions of Jews to the concentration camps.

I did not attend the Eichmann trial, nor did I read about it. When I think about it now, I know that I simply would not have been able to bear hearing the excruciating and detailed testimonies of the many witnesses. This man, this Eichmann, was the Nazi responsible for putting my eighty-three-year-old great-grandmother Ružena on a train to Treblinka.

Of course I was glad that Eichmann was found guilty—how could I not have been? Gideon Hausner, Israel's attorney general, was the lead prosecutor, and he was magnificent in how he conducted and carried out the trial, with a great deal of evidence and human dignity.

I want to share with you what he said at the beginning of the trial:

When I stand before you here, Judges of Israel, to lead the Prosecution of Adolf Eichmann, I am not standing alone. With me are six million accusers. But they cannot rise to their feet and point an accusing finger towards him who sits in the dock and cry: "I accuse." For their ashes are piled up on the hills of Auschwitz and the fields of Treblinka, and are strewn in the forests of Poland. Their graves are scattered throughout the length and breadth of Europe. Their blood cries out, but their voice is not heard. Therefore I will be their spokesman and in their name I will unfold the terrible indictment.

The closest I got to Eichmann's trial was not too long ago, when I visited the Ghetto Fighters' House Museum in Lohamei HaGeta'ot, which is in northern Israel, near Acre. It is a wonderful museum. There, among many other exhibits, is the glass partition that Eichmann sat behind during his trial. It was surreal and, of course, upsetting for me to see it. That was close enough. I can hardly comprehend the things Eichmann was responsible for. And he had the chutzpah to claim that he was just a small cog carrying out the wishes of Hitler. He tried to say he was just a "bureaucrat" and was not responsible or aware of what was happening.

I think that when Israelis heard the testimonies at that trial, they looked at Holocaust survivors with greater empathy and respect. The Eichmann trial helped people be understood not only by their own family stories but also through the stories of many others, which painted a much bigger picture of the horrible things that happened.

In 1985, when I finally told my story to those German high school students, it was a turning point in my life emotionally and personally. It became known in the area where I lived that I was a Holocaust survivor and that I did a pretty good job, I guess, of telling my story. I started receiving invitations to speak to Israeli students in local schools. And these invitations I gladly accepted. I brought along family photos and a couple of maps of the Sudeten to show exactly how and where my family was affected.

It is not unusual for Israeli schoolkids to have had relatives who were in the Holocaust. Israeli kids have heard the stories passed down to them within their families. Slowly, over time, these stories were shared more widely.

Many people don't realize that over half of Jewish Israelis living today did not come from Europe but from North African and Middle Eastern countries, such as Morocco, Libya, Tunisia, and Iraq. The Nazis took actions against the Jews in those places too. Israeli schoolkids start off with more information about the Holocaust than most kids elsewhere do, which makes it easier for me to speak to them. They ask a lot of questions about how I felt and how I survived and what it was like. I think because I was a kid at the time, they can relate to me, being kids themselves.

•-•-•

On Yom HaShoah, many survivors receive invitations to tell their stories at schools and other places. Yom HaShoah is our National Holocaust Remembrance Day in Israel. It takes place in April or May and starts the night before, because in the Jewish tradition, days go from sundown to sundown. When the sun goes down, a lot of people light a special memorial candle called a Yarhzeit candle that burns for twenty-four hours. I usually light two, one for my dad and one for my beloved Grandpa Alfred.

On Yom HaShoah, the whole country goes quiet. It is a very somber day. There are no movies showing or television broadcasting on Israeli channels. Schools are closed, there are no buses, and most businesses are closed. At ten in the morning, in every village, town, and city in Israel, a siren goes off for two minutes. Everybody stops what they are doing, wherever they are, and stands still, bowing their heads. Even cars on the streets and freeways pull over, and the drivers get out of their vehicle and stand with their heads bowed too.

When this happens, I feel sad but also connected to my country because I look around and everyone—that little child there, that mother, that bus driver, that waiter, that motorcycle rider—everyone stops and we are all together, paying our respects to the unthinkable loss of so many innocent lives.

In 2011, a wonderful organization called Zikaron b'Salon was started. Young people all over Israel host Holocaust survivors in their homes to tell their stories on Yom HaShoah. The people at Zikaron b'Salon are well aware that there aren't many Holocaust survivors left alive anymore. Some survivors who are still living are not able to speak and tell their stories because of illness or dementia. It is very sad. And it makes me more determined than ever to keep on going as long as I can because I feel I am speaking now for so many who can't speak.

·◆·

I was eighty-five-years young when I first used social media to tell my story. It was Julie's idea. She explained that a lot of young people all over the world were using social media to do all sorts of things, from dancing to telling jokes to showing how to cook food and more. We knew that our friend Lily Ebert was telling her story of surviving Auschwitz on TikTok, and we were friendly with her great-grandson, Dov. So we thought, Well, Lily was brave enough to try, why not give it a shot?

It was very strange at first because I am used to telling my story the long way—the whole story to the end, or at least one part of it. There were a lot of challenges for me to get used to. For one example, on social media I had to make a video that was maybe one minute long. Sometimes even thirty seconds. Let me tell you, the idea of that was very difficult for me to accept—one minute?

We tried a few things to make that possible for me at my age. I learned that you can edit these videos, which Julie would do, so that if I went on too long, we could use only one small part. And we discovered an app that is like a teleprompter, so we could use that to help me out if I had a lot to say. Julie made it go very slowly so I could keep up with the words.

Julie is very creative, and sometimes she would just show my face looking at the camera and then she would put what I wanted to say as words that you could read. I really think a lot of older people could go on social media to share about their lives if they know about some of these ways to make it easier for themselves.

So with these ways of helping, I was able to tell only small parts of my story. For example, I would show my mother's yellow Star of David and explain how my family and others were forced to wear the badges. Or I made a video about the first wonderful thing I remember after liberation—riding the officers' abandoned horses bareback at Theresienstadt! Another video shows the pendant my father gave my mother right before he was transported to Auschwitz, and I explain what happened to my father.

Later, we did videos with facts about the Holocaust that were not part of my personal experience. For example, one time we made one about Aktion T4, when the Nazis murdered mentally and physically disabled people because they thought people like that were not human like everybody else. As we made videos like this, I found myself learning more and more about the Holocaust. I can't say that was a good feeling.

One day, early on in this whole adventure, we were driving somewhere, and our phones were going *ping ping ping ping ping ping*. Julie checked and it was people "liking" one of our videos. We said, "Oh my God, people are looking at our videos!" That inspired us to keep going. After a while, hundreds of thousands of people were looking at our videos. We had nine million "likes"!

To my utter amazement, I went from being very hesitant to talk about my experience to talking to classrooms of Israeli kids to being on social media essentially talking to millions of people all over the world!

I did wonder and question whether people were really learning about the Holocaust the way they could from a book. But Julie and I agreed that our goal was to get people interested so they would be curious to learn more. We put together a list of books about antisemitism and the Holocaust so that people could go and learn more. These were books that Julie had already read, and some I had read too, and others were books that are highly recommended.

To my surprise, Julie included three "graphic" books that she thought were good books, and she asked me to read them. I had never read a book like that! It's like reading a comic strip, which, I admit, I thought was very strange. But in this way, I read the graphic book version of the *Diary of Anne Frank* and *On Tyranny* by Timothy Snyder. I also read *Maus* by Art Spiegelman. To be honest, I don't like graphic books all that much, although now I can say that I have tried them. I actually thought *Maus* was very clever. In fact, I learned a lot from all three books.

I still cannot believe how many people all over the world express such affection toward me on social media. They say that when they see my videos, it "makes their day" and brings them hope. The feeling this gives me is hard to put into words. I guess you could say that it means quite a lot to me.

I suppose, because of this business with social media, people began to find us and send us emails. I have been on Israeli and German television a number of times, with people putting makeup on my face and fussing over me and cameras pointing at me. Honestly, I really do enjoy it.

Sometimes, neighbors or friends and even complete strangers say, "Hey, I saw you on TV yesterday!" Sometimes I walk down the street or go to the beach and young people (and not-so-young people) say, "Hey, I know you from social media!" It is amazing and I do love and appreciate it. At times, I am in a state of shock.

On Yom HaShoah in the last two or three years, some major Israeli pop stars have come to our house to make videos with me. I had never heard their music or known of them, but before they arrived, Julie showed me their music videos so I would have some idea. She also got me a small speaker that connects to my phone by Bluetooth so I could listen to their music. I love that speaker! Right away, I asked Julie to put my favorite music on there, so I can listen all the time. Of course, my favorite music is Simon & Garfunkel, so I like to listen to them since that brings back so many good memories for me. But I also like a lot of folk music like Pete Seeger and Woody Guthrie. I like music like that very much. But these pop singers were something totally different for me.

Anyhow, when I told my children and grandchildren about who was coming to see me, they could not believe it. I really liked my visit with Stéphane Legar; he is so tall! I taught him a folk dance and he taught me some of his moves. He was wearing crazy clothes, but I loved it. When Static came to visit me, all the kids in the neighborhood found out and went out into the street to meet him. He took pictures with them and signed autographs. I also did a video with Montana Tucker. I didn't know who she was, of course, but then I saw her dance videos. Turns out, she, too, has lost family and relatives in the Holocaust. Montana was in Los Angeles when we did the filming, and I was here in Israel, but her team set a bunch of things up to make it possible, and I had people helping me too. Montana is really a good dancer, in my opinion, and a very nice person.

None of these things would I have ever imagined happening in my lifetime.

I have also been invited to some very formal events. In fact, I was the guest of honor at a gathering hosted by the European Jewish Association (EJA) in Prague. I could not believe it. It was a gathering of diplomats and members of parliament from all over Europe. This group meets every year to discuss issues that affect the Jewish people in Europe. I am sorry to say that a major topic when I attended was antisemitism because it has really gotten much worse. I knew about that from social media and it being on the news, but I will say again that I am quite shocked about it.

I must admit, I was so nervous when it came time to tell my story on the stage. I was looking at all these people in the audience and it was totally overwhelming. Bright lights shone on me and many cameras were filming, and some people sitting in a small glass booth off to the left translated my every word. Here I was, the little boy who had been deported to Theresienstadt from Prague, and now very serious people were listening to every word I was saying—in many languages! I was lucky, though, because I was given something like half an hour to speak, not one minute.

Julie also gave a talk about how we use social media to educate young people about the Holocaust. She has more experience with doing presentations than I do, so for her it's a bit easier. But she admitted that she was nervous too. Julie showed the people some of our videos, and I think she did a great job. I was very proud of her.

Later, there was a very formal dinner and lots of other speeches, and the press was there too. It was another world for me. The next day, I went down for breakfast and at least a dozen people (I didn't, for the most part, know who they were) came over and shook my hand and said very kind things. I had to pinch myself. A couple of days later, a member of the British Parliament made a speech about this event in the British House of Commons. He even mentioned me, Gidon Lev! Wow!

Only one week later, I had an even more amazing experience if that is possible to say. I went from Prague to Dubai in one single week!

The Ministry of Foreign Affairs of Israel heard about me from my being on TV and social media. I guess they liked what they saw because they sent me and Julie both to Dubai, which is in the United Arab Emirates. Not only had I never been to that place, but also I had never even dreamed that it would be possible. We flew on Emirates Airlines, which was just as nice as the advertisements show, believe me. It was very comfortable.

The Israeli consulate took care of Julie and me both during our visit and drove us all around Dubai. We had a lovely hotel and were treated like royalty; we didn't know what to do with ourselves! We saw the Dubai Frame, which is a very tall, golden picture frame right in the middle of Dubai. It is tremendously big and really quite a sight to see.

Julie has a friend in Dubai named Fahad whom she had never met in person. So Fahad came with his whole family to our hotel and treated us to dinner. Fahad was wearing a *kandura*, the long white robe that men in the Emirates wear for special occasions. It looked really comfortable and I wished that I had one! We both enjoyed Fahad's family and even got to know his kids by asking about their interesting lives in Dubai. It was a really enjoyable evening.

We took a lot of pictures while we were there and we visited the highest building in the world, the Burj Khalifa. The elevator ride goes by very quickly because it's a high-speed elevator. Looking around at Dubai from such a height, I was amazed to be in such an interesting place, somewhere I never dreamed I would go.

There is a gentleman there in Dubai, Ahmed Al Mansoori, whom we got to meet. I really was impressed by him. He opened the first exhibit about the Holocaust in the Middle East outside of Israel in a museum he created called the Crossroads of Civilization Museum. I found Mr. Al Mansoori to be well-spoken, and he was very kind to me. I was invited to give a talk about my life right there at his museum.

As excited as I was to visit Dubai, I will admit that I was even more nervous to speak! I am familiar with Prague, but not with Dubai, and at this event I knew there would be some very important people from all over. But I was determined to do my best.

As I was introduced, I stood on the podium and looked out over that audience. There was Julie sitting in the front row, encouraging and supporting me, and I could also see so many important dignitaries and ambassadors and diplomats, some dressed in the formal wear of Arabs. I had never seen so many dignitaries in my life! It was really unforgettable for me, this little boy from Theresienstadt.

On a large screen behind me, we displayed photos of my family. They were normal family pictures, the kind everyone has. I explained to the audience, best I could, what happened to my family members:

My grandfather Fritz, his wife, Elsa, and my mother's half-brother Karel all died in the Warsaw Ghetto. I don't know if they died of starvation or were shot or were sent to Treblinka in the Grosse Aktion. I have the transport papers showing that they were sent to Warsaw from Theresienstadt on transport number AN as prisoners numbered 456, 457, 458 on April 25, 1942. At least they were all together. There are no records after that.

I told the people listening that my father's dad, my grandfather Alfred, died in Theresienstadt and that my great-grandmother Ružena was sent from Theresienstadt to be murdered at Treblinka. I told them that my mother's mom, my grandmother Liesel, was murdered in a place called Izbica, which is in Poland.

I told them how my mother's aunts and uncles from Vienna were sent away only a month after we had arrived in Theresienstadt: Martha was murdered in Riga, which is in Latvia, and the Jews were murdered there by shooting. Robert was murdered in Auschwitz. He was sixty-two years old. Olga died in Maly Trostenets, which is in Belarus today. Emil, along with his wife, took poison rather than allow themselves to be taken away. He was sixty-one. Only my mother's aunt Elsa survived.

I told them that my father's aunt Dora and uncle Gustav were sent to Auschwitz on February 1, 1943.

I told them the story of my father too. My mother said goodbye to him at the train station at Theresienstadt. The train was going east. Somehow, my father managed to throw a small package to my mother, who caught it and ran back to our barracks with it. Inside was a pendant and photograph of my mother that my dad always kept with him. That was in September 1944.

At Auschwitz, my dad was prisoner number B12156. In January 1945, the Nazis began the death marches to evacuate the camps. They were retreating from the coming Russian army. They feared the Russians more than they feared the Allies. At Yad Vashem in Israel, I found the transport papers for my father. He was supposed to be sent from Auschwitz to Buchenwald. They set off on foot on January 17, 1945. But my father didn't make it. He might have collapsed from hunger and weakness and been shot on the side of the road. He might have tried to escape. I will never know for sure. The Russians liberated the camp on January 27, 1945. Had he remained in Auschwitz for ten more days, I might have had a father.

I told them how, all in all, I have twenty-six family members who were murdered by the Nazis. And by the time I was finished doing all that telling, most of the people listening to my story were crying, including me.

•—•—•

In the fall of 2022, I returned to Theresienstadt. Julie and I had gone back two or three times, for different reasons. This time, we went because of Yaniv Rokah, the film director who made *Queen Mimi*. Yaniv, whom I consider to be a very good man and friend, was making a documentary about me!

During that visit, I must tell you, I felt empowered. There I was, so many years later, a free person, an old man even, walking around and remembering things while a film crew was recording it. I saw the place where we kids used to play soccer and I could almost hear the shouts of the kids again. Simply walking down the mostly deserted streets, past different barracks, brought back so many memories. We walked by the barracks where I lived, which is now crumbling down. I learned that it might be demolished and replaced either by housing or a school of some sort.

This might surprise you, but I feel this is the right thing to do. Other barracks at Theresienstadt are very well preserved, and there is a very good museum too. I am sure that if they do demolish the building, they will make good use of the space and leave a marker there as a reminder. Life goes on and we have to move forward.

I played around with a soccer ball with one of my grandsons, Eli, who came with us, and I remembered when some kids and I played soccer with a ball made out of strips of our old clothing and all I could think was "Look at me now—I am here, I have survived!" This little boy, me, who has gone through so much, is making the world just a little bit better today. Just a little bit. And that is more than I could ever have dreamed of or hoped for.

Then, something truly wonderful happened that nobody could have predicted. We were filming near the train tracks, where Jews from all over Europe arrived and where the trains departed to go east. This was the place where all my family was sent to their deaths, so you can imagine I was feeling very emotional. I was putting some wildflowers down on the dilapidated tracks when we noticed, about a hundred yards away, a tour group coming toward us. They had Israeli flags and were pretty noisy. They saw me, Julie, and our camera crew and asked what was going on. I told them that I was a child survivor of the camp and that we were filming a documentary. They surrounded me and asked me lots of questions. Among them was another survivor of Theresienstadt. She was a woman probably about my age and she was wearing a sheitel, which is the wig that some religiously observant Jewish women wear. She didn't say too much to me, but I have noticed that sometimes when I come upon other Holocaust survivors we don't have too much to say to each other. I don't know why that is. Maybe language differences or maybe we're weary of our stories after all these years. But we always do embrace very warmly and that's what we did.

The group had a rabbi with them, presumably their tour leader, and he led them in a religious song. I am not religious, but it was okay. Then I told them that I would like to sing a song that is very special to me and lots of Israelis. It's called "Shir HaEmek." The lyrics were written by a very famous Israeli poet, Nathan Alterman. It's a beautiful song about the Jezreel Valley in Israel, which is the place where I first came to Israel, the place I live now, and the place I will be buried one day.

So, I started singing, and lo and behold, everybody sang along with me! Hearing us all singing "Shir HaEmek" together there, at the place where I and so many others were imprisoned, was a special moment that I won't soon forget.

After a warm goodbye, the people resumed their tour. I thought about my family and the suffering that we and so many others went through. But there we were, so many years later, singing a song of hope and promise.

7

THE LIFE THAT YOU GET

Gidon and Susan, 1999.

M Y ELDEST GRANDSON, NOI, IS A CLOWN. HE WEARS COLOR-
ful costumes, juggles, and does tricks and acrobatics to
entertain children. Not only children, but their parents too,
and he does it all over Israel. It is his profession, and he loves
it. Noi is the eldest son of my son Yanai, who, it seems to me,
only yesterday was a little boy. Noi has a wild head of red hair
and a beard. He looks a little bit like a prophet of some kind,
like Moses incarnate, leading the way!

Noi's two daughters, my great-granddaughters, Ya'ara and Niri, get in on the acrobatics too. They can already balance themselves and do all sorts of amazing tricks with their tiny bodies. In fact, that whole side of the family does something called "acro-balance," which is doing headstands, handstands, and different combinations of those with two, three, even five people together and always landing on their feet with a flourish. It really is quite something to see. At times, when I watch them perform, I am reminded of my first love, Anuška, the little tumbling girl in Theresienstadt who loved to do headstands too.

◦–◦–◦

Not long ago, Julie and I moved to a very special new home. Julie calls it our "Hobbit house" because it's a very cozy cottage tucked in a forest, very high up on a hill. Everywhere I look, I can see the fields of the beautiful Jezreel Valley below and it brings me so much joy. This is where my life in Israel began and this is where it will end.

But it was a difficult move. Julie and I moved from our home in Ramat Gan, which is near Tel Aviv, right in the middle of the most serious, frightening, and deadly war in Israel for fifty years, the war between Israel and Hamas.

When this terrible war broke out, we were doing our packing. The stress, uncertainty, and anguish of the terrible news combined with the daily dashes to our bomb shelter, sometimes two or three times a day with the sirens wailing and explosions—this on top of all the tasks we needed to do in order to move was, at times, almost unbearable. But somehow,

we made it. We had to. We didn't have a choice. We simply
had to keep going.

Shortly after our move, with the terrible war still raging and
the winter rains coming down, it was Hanukkah, the Festival
of Lights. Believe me, it was hard to feel anything close to fes-
tive. But we knew that if we went on with our traditions and
gatherings, it would be a way of holding onto hope for better
days. So we invited my whole family—as many of them who
could join us—up to our little cottage on the hill to kindle the
Hanukkah lights.

All in all, thirty souls came to our home that night to light
the candles and remember, as a family, that we need light and
hope to sustain us in the darkest times.

Noi was there, of course, with his partner, Shai, and little
Niri and Ya'ara.

My third son, Elisha, brought beautiful lights to put up in
the garden and set about grilling all the meat, which he is a
real expert at. Eti, Elisha's wife, and the mother of four of my
grandchildren, brought several delicious cakes that she had
made. Eti's family came to Israel from Morocco in the 1950s.
On Shabbat at Eti's house, I have learned to appreciate and
even come to love the spicy Moroccan food Eti makes, espe-
cially the fish.

My son Yanai came from Kibbutz Mishmar Ha Emek with
an apple cake he made. My son Shaya came from Jerusalem
with my sweet and talented daughter-in-law, Tamar, and my
grandson Ido, who is so smart he built his own computer.
My daughter Hadasa came from Tel Aviv with my son-in-
law Asaf and, of course, my beautiful, talented, and sensitive

granddaughter Yael. Her brother, my grandson Sahar, is in New York studying acting.

For me, to see four generations gathered under one roof celebrating miracles and hope was almost overwhelming. It is times like these that I think of Susan and I miss her. How she would have loved to have been there to see her children and grandchildren and how they have grown. From a young woman in Tel Aviv in love with a cellist to the wife of someone like me, to the grandmother and great-grandmother of such a crowd—I don't think Susan would ever stop smiling!

I did miss my eldest daughter, Maya, who lives in California, and her two children, Eli and Eva, and my youngest son, Asher, who lives in Brussels with his wife, Irina, and my youngest grandchild, Moshé. Nonetheless, seeing most of us together that evening, I couldn't help but be so proud to see how my children have grown and how proud they make me. I thought of everything that I and their mother had gone through for these moments to be possible.

In the Jewish faith there is a blessing called the *shehechayanu*, which is a prayer of thanks that we have made it to this moment, no matter what we have been through. Believe me, I said this blessing on this night. This is how it goes in English:

Blessed are You, L-rd our G-d, King of the Universe, who has granted us life, sustained us and enabled us to reach this occasion.

Together, we sang "Ma'oz Tzur" and danced and ate until we were all completely stuffed. Later, when all my famous latkes had disappeared, and all the wonderful food had been eaten, and the cakes were gone, and the children were tired and ready to go home, Noi the prophet started washing the many dishes. He was being his usual helpful, cheerful, comical self when he noticed that the sink was plugged and the water, instead of going down the drain, was pouring out onto the floor of the kitchen.

Noi picked up the plunger and held it up like a sword. "Come on, Saba! Let's slay the dragon!" Immediately, my kids and grandkids, led by Noi, pitched in. It took a while, but together we fixed the problem, at least temporarily. Before everybody left, my kids and grandkids made sure that my floor was swept and mopped and shiny clean again.

We all have unexpected challenges. It's how we face them that matters. My family chooses coming together to celebrate our traditions and we choose laughter and teamwork too. That makes me so proud and happy.

·•·

I never chose to be born a Jew and I certainly didn't choose to be a victim of the Nazis. As I write this book, antisemitism has raised its head all over the world and horrifyingly so, even in America. And on top of it all, there is this terrible war between Israel and Hamas. For sure, I would have never wanted these terrible and frightening events to happen during my lifetime. And yet they happened and are happening. These are all circumstances that are far beyond my control.

Of course, many people would have wanted to be born somewhere else or be different in some ways. In fact, I wish I was born taller. I wish I was a famous dancer. I wish there was no war and that everybody in the world got along peacefully. I wish that the people I love would never die. I wish I would have had a father.

Yet, I am who I am because of all my experiences—or maybe despite them! The fact is, you don't get the life that you *want*—you get the life that you *get*. If you are very lucky, the life that you get will have many chapters, as I have had. So far, this is the life that I got and I have tried to make the best of it.

•-•

Life can be totally unpredictable, even when we try to have a routine and do all the normal things. We get up in the morning and brush our teeth, drink our first cup of coffee or tea, and make a list of things to get done this day, then we go off to work, hoping it will be a good day that will give us satisfaction. And yet life can throw us a curveball at any moment. Some of those moments, we never forget.

One such moment came in 1970, after a painful and bitter separation from my first wife. We had worked out a custody arrangement that was less than ideal, to say the least, but I had no idea just how wrong it could go. Sometime in June 1970, I left Yanai, who was two and a half years old, for a weekend visit with his mother and sister, Maya, in Jerusalem.

When I went back to pick him up, I found an envelope pinned to the door of the apartment. Inside the envelope was a key and a note. The note had only five words: "We have gone to America."

100

I took the key out of the envelope and opened the door, not knowing what I would find. What I saw shocked me. I felt as if I had been struck by a thunderbolt. The apartment that only two days earlier had been the home of my ex-wife, her partner, and my daughter was totally barren.

I will never, for as long as I live, forget that moment. It is hard for me to think of it, even today. I felt totally betrayed. We had had an agreement.

First, I cried and then I banged my head against the wall. I was emotionally broken. I slid down to the floor. Hadn't I lost my entire family once before? Was I being punished a second time in my lifetime? How would I cope? What could I do? Who would help me? I didn't even have an address or a phone number. Nothing. I felt, in that moment, totally empty, as if something inside me had been destroyed beyond repair.

But somehow, even feeling such anguish, I knew that I didn't have the privilege of letting the shock, anger, and sorrow overcome me. I tried to calm myself down and think.

I returned to my home on Kibbutz Zikim. As soon as I arrived, people asked me where my son was because, of course, I always returned with him. I could hardly answer their questions in my state of distress and shock. Somehow it occurred to me that I should go see the kibbutz psychologist and the kibbutz secretary and tell them what had happened. We discussed various options and solutions to help me get my children back to Israel. As we did so, I began to feel something stirring in me again—hope. As I thought about doing something to repair this terrible situation, I could feel my energy slowly returning to me.

Within ten days, I landed in the United States and began my search for the children. There were many stops along the way and mistakes and good things too. Ultimately, I brought only my son back to Israel, and I had to live with this painful conclusion for the rest of my life. I certainly wish I had done so many things differently and I wish my ex had too. But so many years later, that is water under the bridge. Despite the fact that their parents truly messed up, our son and daughter both grew up to be very fine people, one in America and one in Israel.

--◆--

Yes, life has thrown me a number of curveballs. Sometimes one after the other. It was 1992 and I was happily remarried and raising Yanai, Hadasa, Shaya, Elisha, and Asher with Susan. One day, my phone rang. It was my mother, who was living in Toronto on her own, since my stepfather Jus had passed away ten years earlier. My mother told me that in the next twenty-four hours, she was going to have a major colon operation. I was shocked. My mother had never told me that she had cancer!

I got on a plane the same day and arrived on time to be present during her surgery. Thank God, she made it okay. I stayed there in Toronto for the next three weeks helping my mother recover. I wanted to understand what she had gone through and what might come next, so I read all the pamphlets and booklets at the hospital about colon cancer. After reading all this, I had a terrible realization. I, too, was having symptoms that could indicate colon cancer. I can't tell you how scared I felt.

After I made sure my mother was okay, I returned to Israel and immediately went to my doctor. After a colonoscopy procedure, I discovered that, yes, I had colon cancer. Susan and I were both devastated to receive this news.

Within days I was on the operating table. After the surgery, the doctor informed me that my cancer was stage four cancer. I needed to undergo chemotherapy for the next year if I wanted to live.

At first, after the operation, it was not so bad. I recovered pretty well. But then I started the chemo treatments, which took place every two weeks. I would receive my treatment, then go home and rest for a couple of days, overcome with fatigue and nausea. Then I went straight back to work. Over time, doing this twice a month for several months, it became harder and harder. Anyone who has had a serious illness and had to undergo treatment for a long period of time will understand how exhausting, demoralizing, and debilitating treatments can be.

Halfway through my treatments, I became disillusioned and depressed. I was drained in every way. I had no energy, no hope, and no sense of humor, which is not like me.

A lot of people call me a "rascal," but believe me, during that time, I was like someone else altogether. Even I didn't recognize myself; neither did Susan. I did not want to continue the treatment. I was prepared to give up and let cancer win. In fact, had it not been for Susan, who spent long hours talking with me and helping me overcome this serious glitch in my character, I probably would have given up and wouldn't be here today. Susan reminded me again and again that it was not like me to give up. She reminded me of all the adventures we'd had together and how much we had overcome.

•◆•

In 2002, to my total disbelief, I was diagnosed with cancer yet again. This time it was bladder cancer. Little did I know that the treatments I had to undergo would last for seven long years.

For my treatments, I went to a hospital in Nazareth. There are three hospitals there, the Italian hospital, the French hospital, and the English hospital. Doctors and nurses work there, of course, but also nuns from the different Christian denominations. Elisha was born in the Italian hospital. I once had a hernia operation at the Italian hospital, and my doctor was a Reform rabbi from India!

For my bladder cancer treatments, I went to the English hospital. My doctor was Dr. Basel Fahum, who tried as hard as he could to stop the cancer. I had to go about every three months and check in to the hospital to recover from the procedure for two to three days. So you can imagine, doing this four times a year for seven years, I got to know the nurses and my doctor very well!

First, I had to receive a spinal injection to completely numb me from the waist down. My mind wanted to move my legs, but my legs couldn't respond. It was a strange and frightening feeling even though it was necessary. Then Dr. Fahum would go into my bladder and clean up the persistent cancer by scraping or burning it off. Afterward, I went into the recovery room and waited patiently for the feeling to return to my legs. Dr.

Fahum saved my life and I am forever grateful to him and to all the nurses and doctors at the English hospital.

Looking back, I think I was better able to believe that I might recover from cancer the second time because I had experienced it before, a few years earlier. I sort of knew what to expect emotionally. Of course, part of me did fear that I wouldn't get lucky twice. My children and especially my grandkids were fearful when they saw me in the hospital. They thought I would not survive. It was upsetting for me to see them feel so frightened and, to be honest, it gave me some doubts, yet I also saw how much they cared and wanted me to get better.

In the end, the cancer could not be stopped and resulted in me having to have my bladder removed, which left me with new plumbing. But I managed to survive.

I must have given the impression to my family and friends that I am a fighter and that I don't give up because a while ago, when I didn't feel good, Julie got scared and called my son Shaya to ask his advice. Shaya said, "Julie, it's Aba. Aba doesn't die." That made me smile because in some ways it's actually the truth.

·-•-·

You might think that you have nothing in common with me, this old guy, a Holocaust survivor, but you are wrong. I have had many challenges in my life and I am sure that you have too. None of us can avoid going through difficult times. They happen to everybody. Some of them are your fault, most are not. Many things you cannot control at all. But these challenges don't weaken you, they strengthen you because they allow you to see the world from a new perspective. And in many ways, challenges prepare you for other tough times that may come your way—and don't worry, they will come!

I think because in my formative childhood years I had so much taken away from me and so little that I could rely on that I became very practical. Whatever was in front of me was in front of me. If there were a couple of rotten potatoes lying on the ground on the other side of a fence, I would find a sharp stick to try to get them. If the Nazis said, "Here, carry this bread," then I carried the bread and pinched a few bites. I didn't ask, "Why is this happening to me? This isn't fair." I just made the best of what I had. So even when bad things happen to me today, I think to myself, "Okay, what can I do about this? How can I make things better?"

·•·

Here in Israel, before the war, we had protests every week, all over the country. Thousands and thousands of us Israelis took to the streets to protest the weakening of our fragile democracy. I went as often as I could. I made a few protest signs, giving each one a lot of thought. I used markers and poster paper. For sticks to hold them up, I found leftover wood on the sidewalk and hammer and nails. One of my signs was so big it needed two sticks to hold it up! My picture turned up in a lot of newspapers and even the *Washington Post*.

I went in the summer, in the heat, and I went in the winter, when it rained. Julie and I worked out a system so that I could be right in the center of the protests along with everybody else fighting for democracy. We left our home early so we could find parking so I didn't have to walk far and could save my energy for the march. We made sure we brought water and that we wore comfortable shoes. We worked out places where I could sit and rest, still holding my sign, so I didn't get too tired.

After all that, after months and months, the whole thing collapsed because of the war. It was so disheartening. But believe me, when it is possible to get out there again to make my voice heard, I will be there. I will march and protest and hope and act and speak until my dying day because I believe that taking action matters.

But I also believe in being very honest, and truth be told, I am more than a little worried these days. I don't see clear answers to some of the problems going on with climate change, wars, populism, and immigrant crises. Just like everyone, of course, I want to know how we will solve these problems. I don't want them to get worse.

It's natural to want to know what the solutions will be so we can have hope. That is why it's so tempting for some people to make things black and white as if they know exactly what the answer to a problem is. But most of the time, it takes time to figure things out. Sometimes a lot of time. In my life, I have learned that even when I couldn't see the solutions, they were there, all along, just waiting to be found at the right time in the right way. In fact, sometimes there is not one, big solution but lots of small ones that work together, one by one and little by little.

·–•–·

Emily Dickinson wrote a poem with these words:

> *"Hope" is the thing with feathers—*
> *That perches in the soul—*
> *And sings the tune without the words—*
> *And never stops—at all—*

These words are written very beautifully, of course, but I allow myself to question them a little bit. I don't think it's true that hope is always there within us. It can be extinguished in a second, just like a candle. In fact, if someone tells you that they are always hopeful and always positive, they aren't being entirely honest. But in the same way that hope can be blown right out, like a candle, it can also be rekindled just like that, with the tiniest spark of encouragement. We have to look for those little sparks of hope and encouragement, and if we can't find them for ourselves, maybe we can be a spark of hope for someone else. We truly never do know what can happen in the future—maybe even today.

As I write this, yes, there is a terrible war going on all around me. But there are other things too. I have my beloved family with me, and I have a loving partner in Julie. I am fairly healthy, I still am alert, and I continue to learn and do things. I have a big and green garden that I like to take care of, plenty of things to fix and improve, and I even have three cats. I have seen bad times come and go, and good times too. This is the life I got and I consider myself very lucky.

Recently, I read a book called *Hope in the Dark*, by Rebecca Solnit, and it was truly my kind of book! I think I marked up almost every page. One quote stood out to me: "What we dream of is already present in the world." I fully go with that because, to me, hard times are like hide-and-seek—where is the solution, where is the hope? We can never give up looking for these things because they are just waiting to be found.

8
BEARING WITNESS TO HISTORY

Gidon with Auschwitz survivor Menachem
Haberman in 2022.

ACCORDING TO THE KABBALAH, WHICH IS A KIND OF JEWISH
mysticism, when God created the world, it was totally
whole and perfect. But then it got broken and all the pieces
rained down and mixed together. According to this story,
today, it is our job, or even responsibility, to repair the world,
to make it whole again. This is something we Jews call *tikkun
olam*. Repairing the world. *Tikkun olam* can mean something
like doing acts of *chesed*—kindness—or it can mean getting

involved in social justice activities. It's basically about making the world better by fixing what needs to be fixed in whatever way that we can.

Telling my story of surviving the Holocaust doesn't change the past or fix the world, but I do feel that it might just help make this world better because I can share a part of history as I experienced it with my own eyes and ears instead of something you read in a book. I can also be an example for other people who might just share their stories of suffering, too, so that they can heal and feel better and maybe even prevent others from suffering in the same way.

•◆•

When I was a kid in a concentration camp, I really had no idea why I was there. I just did my best to survive. That was all I could do. Everything was totally confusing. I didn't understand what being Jewish meant or why the Nazis hated us so much. I was simply too young. Later, I learned that some prisoners did carry on with observing the Jewish holidays, when and if they could, but I have no memories of taking part in that. Had I been able to grow up in a normal way, I am sure I would have learned much more from my family about being Jewish and what that meant for them.

When I came to Israel in 1959, I was very interested in my Jewish heritage but in a secular way, mostly, based on the seasons and the harvest. There were a lot of other Israelis in those days who felt the same way, and there still are today. For me, this approach of connecting to my Jewish heritage is very satisfying, although from time to time I have read or discussed

Bible stories and parables or the teachings of rabbis and I do find some interesting themes and lessons that I am grateful for because they enrich my life.

I am happy to say that Susan and I very much raised our kids to be proud to be Jewish and to express that pride through art and being in nature. Just this past Hanukkah, my granddaughter Orin made a beautiful Hanukkia from a pine branch. Each little candle holder was made from a pine cone that she hollowed out and put a candle in. I was so proud to see that. The pine cone doesn't fall far from the tree! Ha!

When I was living on Kibbutz Hazorea, we celebrated the wonderful harvest festivals that have roots in ancient Jewish history. For religious Jews, there are a lot of prayers and songs to celebrate these holidays, but for us kibbutzniks, it was a way of gathering in gratitude for the hard work we had done and the crops we harvested as a result. I have a feeling that the feeling was exactly the same thousands of years ago when harvesting crops was so important to survival. In fact, in the Bible, Shavuot is called the Festival of Reaping. In more modern times, religious Jews celebrate Shavuot as the time that God gave the Jews the Torah. So it's a very special holiday, whether you are religious, secular, or a little of both.

On kibbutz, Shavuot is a big celebration. Everyone gathers in the fields and we work to help bring in the harvest and we dance and sing songs and the children play. I have many fond memories of Shavuot, except one: I was given the chance to organize the Shavuot festival on Kibbutz Hazorea and I had all the dances planned and the music chosen and absolutely everything organized—and it rained. We had to cancel the entire celebration. Imagine two hundred people, all ready to celebrate and sing and dance, running to their homes and getting soaked to the skin!

．◆．

I'm much more aware today of my Jewish heritage and the wisdom, teachings, writings, and history that brought us to where we are now than I was at any other point in my life. I think that's part of growing older, or at least it is for me. You realize and appreciate all the things that made you who you are.

When I speak, I feel responsible to do a good job and be very accurate because I am not only telling my story and that of my family but also, in some ways, speaking for six million Jews and millions of others who cannot bear witness for themselves. I think of what Gideon Hausner said at the beginning of Eichmann's trial: "I will be their spokesman." So that is why I have read and studied much more about the Holocaust when I went on social media than I ever did before.

Having more knowledge about the Holocaust is, at times, heartbreaking. For example, I knew that the older people in Theresienstadt suffered terribly, but when I read the details of their conditions in H. G. Adler's book *Theresienstadt 1941–1945: The Face of a Coerced Society*, it affected me strongly.

Adler was in Theresienstadt for two and a half years. He was sent to Auschwitz about the time my father was, in the fall of 1944. His wife and mother were murdered there immediately upon their arrival. After he was liberated, Adler made it his business to go back and document what went on in Theresienstadt. I can imagine that collecting this information was painful but also empowering for him since he had suffered too.

Adler carefully documented everything in Theresienstadt, even down to the amount of calories allotted to the prisoners based on whether they worked or were in a different category, like us children and the older people. The older people got the least calories. The documentation Adler got shows what food was ordered for the camp, how many kitchens there were, and so on. In the lists of the food brought in, the two biggest things were potatoes and bread. Fodder beets, which we also call mangold, were given to us a lot in soups. Fodder beets are usually used to feed livestock, so you can see the Nazis were trying to spend as little as possible to keep us alive on the bare minimum. A lot of our food was rotten when we received it. I remember the black potatoes very clearly. We were so hungry that we ate them anyway.

From Adler's book, I learned that there was a lot of corruption with the food, from the suppliers to the organizers, to the people who cooked it, prepared it, and served it. For example, the Nazis ordered food for the camp from suppliers, who would then fill those orders with food that was already rotten or with "meat" that was made from the scraps they would normally throw away. The people organizing the food in the camp would distribute more food to people of higher standing than others. People who worked in the kitchen, as my mother did for a time, would steal little pieces of food and put it in their pockets to take home to their children. Not everybody got the same thing. The elderly people got the least calories unless they had someone working in the kitchen who might do them a favor, in which case they might get a few extra bites.

Everyone struggled to survive in an atmosphere of such desperation, want, and cruelty, and this situation made people see each other as competition for food and so on. Being prisoners in such uncertain, frightening conditions made people do whatever they had to do to stay alive. That is something about the concentration camps, no matter where they were or what their conditions were, that adds to the inhumane cruelty of it all. It made people act in ways that they normally never would. Then the Nazis could say, "Look at how they act toward each other. These are humans?"

For me, thinking about this and seeing these facts in black and white, about the diseases, the conditions, the very few calories allotted—none of which I understood at the time—causes me to realize more clearly how much everybody suffered, including my beloved grandfather Alfred. Today, I am a grandfather of fifteen grandchildren, and as I feel and notice my body aging and my energy waning, I think of my grandpa at my age, hungry all the time, cold at night, not having the medications he might have needed...this is very painful for me to think about.

--•--

Many people may not realize that survivors of inhumanity and suffering experience their trauma over and over again: once as it was happening and then again when they learn more of the facts, and then again every time they tell their story.

People who share their stories of pain and suffering of whatever kind are brave. People who feel they cannot share their stories yet should be respected too because everybody is different. I didn't share my story for decades, so I understand.

I have met many Israeli Holocaust survivors at Beit Theresienstadt, where we sometimes gather. We are always happy to see each other, but we don't usually talk about what happened. We prefer to think about our lives after the Holocaust. We all have our stories, and each one is sad and different. We would rather talk about our grandchildren.

I met Dita Krauss, who also survived Theresienstadt, at the Czech Embassy in Tel Aviv, which also holds nice events for us Czech Jews from time to time. There is a book about Dita called *The Librarian of Auschwitz* that I hope you read. Dita and I have never spoken to each other about our experiences, but we did take a picture together.

Menachem Haberman is a very fine man, and through no fault of his own, when I am with him, I feel sad. Menachem is about eight years older than me and also Czech. He was on the same death march as my father, on January 17, 1945. Menachem was eighteen years old, but somehow, he managed to survive the death march only to be sent to other camps like Buchenwald. I don't think Menachem ever met my father, but that they went through the same ordeal together and he survived and my father didn't makes the pain of the loss of my father almost unbearable.

I was introduced to Menachem by Erez Kaganovitch, a talented photographer from Tel Aviv. Erez did a fantastic photography project called Humans of the Holocaust. He met, heard the stories, and took photos of many survivors, including me. Erez made sure that each photograph showed the personality of the survivor, to show them as they are today. I think his photographs are just wonderful.

I was still working delivering flowers when Erez took a photo of me with a lot of flowers around me. It was his idea. Then Julie made a nice winter scarf for me in bright colors and I put that on too.

I also met Yehuda Bacon in his home in Jerusalem. He is a famous Israeli artist, also Czech, who survived Theresienstadt and Auschwitz. Yehuda was born six years before me, in 1929. We did speak about Theresienstadt when we met, and I enjoyed that experience because, among other reasons, to be surrounded by Yehuda's amazing artwork was unforgettable but also because Yehuda reminded me of the German word for mica—the mineral that so many in Theresienstadt had to process for the German war effort. The word was *glimmer*. What a sweet-sounding word in such an awful situation.

Somehow, it was important for me to remember that word and it was nice to hear Yehuda say it because he understood the circumstances. My father was mining it and my mother was processing it; because she processed enough of it, she and I were not sent east. It's so strange to think this mineral, mica, this "glimmer," is central to why I am alive, here, today.

I hope that we all stay healthy and live a long time, but the truth is that we Holocaust survivors, the last generation old enough to remember what happened, are coming to the ends of our lives. That's natural, that's what happens in life. But I hope that makes people think about how our memories can be preserved and used to teach coming generations.

Based on the antisemitism I see today, and the Holocaust denial I have seen on social media, I think it is clear we have to do better than we have in the past. There are many fine Holocaust memorial museums, but most young people don't go to museums these days.

That is one of the reasons I agreed to have an exhibit about me in the Voices of the Forgotten Holocaust Museum in Fortnite. I was not aware of Fortnite, or video games like it; I was born far before that time! But when Luc Bernard approached me about showing pictures and information about my life, I thought, Why not? It was actually fun to help create and I hope many people "visit" me there.

Sometimes on social media, people comment that they visited Dachau or Auschwitz and it changed them forever. I think that's so important, but the reality is that most people live too far away from a former concentration camp to visit those memorials and stand in the place where it happened.

The whole topic of Holocaust survivors and Holocaust education has evolved over the years. It wasn't like the war finished, then five years later people started building museums and Holocaust memorial centers. No. It took society a decade or two just to begin to face this horrifying past or even talk about it because dealing with it is so bloody difficult. It is only in the past few decades that many nations are beginning to look at their past and think of it in new ways. How we teach history is always changing and that is necessary and a part of life.

"*Pravda vitezi*" is a famous Czech saying. It means "the truth will prevail," and I fully go with that. I don't believe that the Holocaust will be totally forgotten. But we have to find better ways to teach about it and other atrocities and wrongs and use this knowledge so that we never have to teach about genocides in the future.

I read in the newspaper some while back that large numbers of young people in America and in Europe were not able to name a single concentration camp. That is very upsetting, of course. However, I also learned that the same is true for many other historical events.

For example, many American kids do not know basic facts about the US Civil War and slavery in America. Many do not know the full story of the Native American Indians in the United States. But you can probably make the same statement about many young people in many countries and the historical events that, for some reason, they do not know much about. I don't know what kids in France know about Napoleon, for example.

We really need to take a hard look at what has gone wrong here, because we will all pay the consequences. In some ways, we are already paying the consequences of this historical amnesia.

The fact is, it isn't just the Holocaust but also many other atrocities, hatreds, and injustices that need to be remembered and taught about in better ways. We can be upset that young people don't know many facts or we can be determined to teach them in better ways. I choose to be determined. I happen to love young people and I believe in them and in the future. It is the older generation who needs to do better! We have to be more creative.

·•·

A lot of people are overcome when they meet me and, I'm sure, other Holocaust survivors. They get very emotional. I enjoy the hugs and the appreciation, but sometimes it feels strange because I am not a hero of any kind. At least I don't feel like one. I just tried to stay alive and I was lucky enough to do so, with the help of my mother. I was just a little boy who didn't want to die.

Sometimes I feel as if I am seen only as a survivor, not as the hard worker, husband, father, grandfather, and even great-grandfather that I am. I want people to know that I have accomplished many things, like raising a large family and plowing the fields of the Jezreel Valley, milking two hundred cows a day, tap and folk dancing, and just living this thing we call life!

Having said that, of course there were psychological effects from the Holocaust that I carry with me to this day. I developed a lifelong dislike of authority because the people who were the "authorities" in my childhood were not just brutal and unfeeling—they were liars. They lied about everything. So I think that made me a bit rebellious and I do challenge things. Even today, I take very little at face value; I check out things on my own and I question things a lot. I realize this sometimes annoys people, but it is how I am.

Also, I do remember, when my kids were small, being very insistent that they finish the food on their dinner plates, and I was sometimes hard on them if they wasted things. I have managed, over time, to be much more relaxed about things like this, but I still have a hard time throwing food away.

•◆•

Telling my story is not easy, but it also affects me in positive ways. It makes me feel empowered because what was taken from us Jews and so many others was our very humanity. And there was nothing we could do about it. Yes, there were a number of instances of resistance and rebellion, but they weren't enough. We were powerless. So in a way, I feel as if I am restoring our humanity by telling our stories.

Telling my story also helps me feel stronger and better as a person because it is a way of facing my past and dealing with the pain and transforming it to something good for people today. From my story, people can learn something about history, and I hope they can also learn something about themselves.

•◆•

When my daughter Hadasa was studying to be an architect, she made beautiful hanging mobiles, some of which I have to this day. Each one is so delicate and so perfectly balanced. One day, a strong wind blew one of her beautiful mobiles down. I was so sad, I loved it so. Carefully, I picked up the pieces and brought them to Hadasa, hoping she could fix it.

A few months went by and then one day, she gave it back to me, all repaired. It was perfectly balanced, elegant, and in harmony, with every beautiful piece there, even if I could still see a chip or two.

I tell you this not only because I love my daughter and her creations but also because it shows that broken things can be repaired. We are all survivors, in one way or another. We all live through heartache, illness, and losing loved ones. We all live through bad days and uncertain times and upheaval in our lives. Some of us have even lived through terrible physical and emotional violence and abuse.

It takes a great deal of time, courage, and support to put the pieces of our heart, soul, and body back together. There might be a chip or two, where things hurt us and even changed us, but that only makes us more of what we are—complicated, beautiful, flawed human beings.

9

SPEAKING OUT AGAINST ANTISEMITISM AND HATRED

(*Left to right*) Gidon's great-grandmother, Rosa (Ružena); his grandfather, Fritz; his mother, Doris; and his father, Ernst. Circa 1934.

"YOU ARE A LIAR! YOU LIE!"

A person left this comment on one of my social media videos. I thought, I am a LIAR? Really, I'm a liar? I really, really wish this *was* a lie. Because if it was a lie, I would have a father, grandfathers, grandmothers, uncles, aunts, and cousins. Why would anyone lie about such a thing?

But I would be liar if I didn't speak honestly here about the antisemitism I have seen on social media and how it makes me feel. To be honest, it makes me so livid, I can hardly express it. But I am also sad. I did not realize how much it had come back. After everything that has happened, how can people question whether the Holocaust really happened or make jokes about it?

For me, it's incomprehensible. Usually, Julie deletes the really nasty comments so that I do not have to see them. But sometimes I do see them and, yes, it is very painful and unbelievable for me to see people say such lies and speak so cruelly about what happened to my family and millions of others. It really makes me wonder how those who have grown up with privilege and peace can be so cruel. I do not understand this.

There is so much of this antisemitism on our social media accounts that Julie became involved with a program at Hebrew University that studies online antisemitism. I think it makes Julie feel better to be doing something about it. She doesn't share too many details with me, but I get the picture. Let's just say that people are getting creative with how they express antisemitism, more now than ever before. They use emojis and even certain numbers to say that they hate Jews. But most of the time they use ordinary words to call me a liar or say that Jews control the whole world and have all the money. I think to myself, "If we Jews control the whole world, we must be doing a pretty terrible job because too many people still hate us!"

•◆•

Some people say that antisemitism is the oldest hatred in the world. I'm not sure which hatred is oldest, but it's been around a long time. I learned something interesting lately: The word *antisemitism* was introduced only in the late 1800s! I don't know what people called it before then, but some people today just call it "Jew hatred." To be honest, I think it might be easier for us to identify it and do something about it if we just call it "hate" because that's what it is, pure and simple. Some people hate anyone who is different and who seems to call into question their beliefs and ways of thinking.

There was a period of time on social media when I made a lot of videos in support of the LGBTQIA community and happily so. I had to learn a lot about it, of course, since I am not part of that community, but when I saw what was being directed at them, I felt I had to say something.

Rabbi Jonathan Sacks said: "The hate that begins with the Jews never ends with the Jews." People don't seem to understand that hate is like a cancer—it will go wherever it can. I don't know why, but when a society is under stress, the Jews are usually the first target, but Rabbi Sacks is right, it never ends there. We only need to look at history to see this.

Some while ago, Julie and I went to Lidice, which is a small village not far from Prague. It was on one of our visits to the Czech Republic. During WWII, there was a terrible massacre at Lidice.

In 1941, about three months before my family and I were sent to Theresienstadt, Hitler appointed Reinhard Heydrich the Deputy Reich Protector of the Protectorate of Bohemia and Morava. Heydrich was a real psychopath, very evil. But

in May 1942, some members of the Czech resistance assassi-
nated him.

Hitler was furious because he considered Heydrich his
right-hand man and a friend. There's even a photograph of
Hitler comforting Heydrich's children at his funeral. So Hitler
decided that the Nazis would hunt down whoever had killed
Heydrich. They practically went from door to door through-
out Prague, arresting and murdering people they thought
might have been involved. These were non-Jewish people, by
the way, just ordinary Czechs who were trying to survive with
the Nazis in control of their country.

Finally, the Nazis got the idea that whoever had killed Hey-
drich or someone who had helped in his assassination was in
the village of Lidice. I am not sure they had any proof. But
they went there one day and massacred practically everybody
in the village. The way they were massacred was just so bru-
tal. I actually don't want to describe it. You can search for it
online. The Nazis did this to many villages in Europe. Mur-
dered, massacred, and destroyed people they thought had
betrayed them. I went to the museum there in Lidice and I
was very moved by what I saw.

The Nazis had a long list of non-Jewish people they per-
secuted or murdered, including "nonconformists," alcoholics,
prostitutes, vagrants, and others they called "asocials." They
had all kinds of badges that prisoners had to wear, like the
pink triangle for gay people, a green triangle for criminals, a
red one for political prisoners, and so on.

The Nazis took over Europe like a wildfire and they burned
it to the ground. Nobody was safe from their evil and wrath.

I think the lesson here—and I'm not sure we've learned it—is that if you support a movement that singles someone else out, believe me, in time, that person will also be you. My advice is to stop and think if you hear intolerance, hate, and blame directed at anyone else—and especially if it's a group of people that is different from you. Pay extra attention then, because it's easy to be manipulated. And if you don't speak out, you are inviting it to your own door in the end.

•◆•

As I write this, the antisemitism I have seen on social media has spread all over the place. I am seeing it in the news, with attacks and vandalism against Jews happening all over the world.

If you ask me what it is like to see this, since I already lost my entire family in the Holocaust, well, it is frighteningly terrible. If my mother were alive, I don't think she could believe it. We thought that when the war ended and the Nazis were defeated and punished, the world had finally learned a lesson. I am very sorry to say that we were wrong. On the one hand, I am in shock and disbelief. But as a Jew, I am also not surprised.

It doesn't seem to matter what Jews say or do, there is always someone who makes up stories about how the Jews are trying to take everything over. During WWII, people said that the Jews were Communists; therefore, they were the enemy. Other people said they were capitalists, so they were the enemy. These are two opposite things, yet people accused the Jews of being one or the other. And this goes back a very long time.

People accused the Jews of killing Jesus when it was the Romans that did away with him. They accused the Jews of poisoning the water wells or bringing disease to villages when these were just natural occurrences.

This totally irrational hatred of Jews takes one form or another and it changes with the times. In the past few decades, people have said that Jews control the media, the banks, and Hollywood. One political woman in America, I can't remember her name, said the Jews controlled the weather with space lasers. I couldn't believe my ears.

Today, some people criticize Israel far above and way beyond the way they criticize other places. I think this is something to think about carefully. Israel deserves a lot of criticism, and I am first and foremost to be a part of that. I have put as much of my energy as I can into protesting against the government in Israel and this terrible situation in the West Bank.

A couple of years ago, I went out at something like three in the morning with a can of spray paint and painted slogans on some political billboards that I didn't agree with. A photograph of my handiwork was in the newspaper the next day. Julie got upset with me because I could have gotten arrested or hurt, but I feel that I have a right and an obligation to make my voice heard as an Israeli and a Jew when I see something wrong that my country is doing. One time, many years ago, I purposely went to see that lunatic Meir Kahane speak so I could speak out against him. There I was, surrounded by hundreds of his supporters, and I began heckling him and challenging the garbage that he was saying. Immediately, I was surrounded by big thugs. Luckily, the police came on time and whisked me out of there.

Israel has been my home since 1959, and I could make a long list of things I am proud of and a long list of things that absolutely break my heart about Israel. And I am not alone in this.

In Israel, we are not so far from Syria, Sudan, Yemen, and Saudi Arabia. I read and hear about terrible, heartbreaking things that happen in those places. But I do not see people reacting anywhere close to what they say about Israel. I think that it should make anyone stop and think very hard about double standards and prejudice. I think this is something people need to discuss carefully.

.-.

"The Nazis were socialists!" This is another crazy thing I see on social media. The Nazis weren't socialists. This is a basic fact. The Nazi Party was called the National Socialist German Workers' Party, but their movement was not related to socialism at all. Nazis hated socialism and communism almost as much as they hated the Jews. But they were master manipulators, so they gave themselves a name that sounded acceptable and maybe even positive. I am sure that many Nazis, were they alive today, would laugh in scorn at those saying that they were socialists.

The very first Nazi concentration camp, Dachau, was established in 1933 and the first prisoners the Nazis rounded up were trade union leaders, communists, and social democrats.

Now you might ask why the Jews were not yet rounded up into that camp. That was because the Nazis were still consolidating their power and they needed to get rid of all political opposition so they could do what they wanted.

Once, when Julie and I were traveling in Europe, we spent some time in Munich, which was the birthplace of Nazism. We saw the place where the Beer Hall Putsch happened in 1923, when Hitler tried to overthrow the government. Let me tell you, standing there in Munich, I could almost see the torches of the Nazis and hear their shouts echoing off the buildings. A little later, we went to the Königlicher Hirschgarten, which is the biggest biergarten in Munich. Under the tall chestnut trees, so many people were drinking huge steins of German beer. There were musicians playing Bavarian folk music *oompah oompah* with their tubas and other instruments. It was so crowded and there was so much gaiety, but somehow I felt so uncomfortable. I looked around at all the happy people and wondered if their grandparents had been Nazis. I wondered if people could tell I was a Jew. It was very loud, but I felt alone and vulnerable as a Jew in the place that started Hitler's career.

On that trip, we paid a visit to Dachau, which is very close to Munich. What a godforsaken place. There were those words again—ARBEIT MACHT FREI—over the gate.

It was a very windy and cold day, but the sun was shining. Julie and I walked through the camp, side by side, looking at the places where the huge barracks used to be. We saw the electrified fence surrounding the camp and learned that many people tried to throw themselves against it to end their suffering. There were watchtowers and lights every few meters.

Being there was extremely difficult. Dachau was built only for one purpose. To torture, work to death, or kill enemies of the Nazis.

•◆•

If you consider Nazis the most evil people who ever existed, you wouldn't be wrong, but then you better understand exactly who and what they were before you compare anything else to them.

During the COVID pandemic, "antivaxxers" said that they were being persecuted the same way the Nazis persecuted the Jews. Some of them even wore the yellow star to make their point. That made my blood boil. Not only was it disrespectful, it was just plain stupid. The Nazis made us Jews wear yellow Stars of David to single us out for humiliation and isolation before they rounded us up and tried to murder as many of us as they could. Governments that required vaccinations were trying to save lives. It was the opposite of what those ignorant people were trying to say. This is what happens when you don't know or understand history. It's dangerous. If we say something like being mandated to get a shot is just like the persecution of the Jews or that leftists are like Nazis, then we have totally lost our way. How can we fight for what is right if we no longer know what is right or wrong, true or false?

We all have to take responsibility for this lack of knowledge of basic history. Maybe we need to educate our educators. Something is very wrong.

•◆•

One of the family photos that I have is of my family in 1934. In the picture, my great-grandmother Rosa is with her son, my grandfather Fritz, and his daughter, my mother, Doris, and my father, Ernst. Lest I forget, I am there in the photo too, inside my mom's tummy! They are strolling along the promenade next to the Teplá River that flows through Karlovy Vary, arm in arm, smiling happily, enjoying a lovely afternoon.

I look at that picture now and I think to myself, this was late 1934, Hitler was already on the rise. How could my family look so relaxed, as if they were totally safe, when only a few hundred kilometers away terrible things were already happening, as if it had nothing to do with them? Why didn't my family do anything? If they had, my life would have been totally different.

But a little while ago, I read a book called *The Oppermanns* by Lion Feuchtwanger and it helped me understand a little better how people try to go about their ordinary lives and ignore warning signs. Feuchtwanger wrote the book in 1933 while the Nazis were rising to power. It's the story of a Jewish family living in Germany only a year before my family photo was taken. In *The Oppermanns*, the family notices small changes, like people don't want to do business with them or the lessons at their son's school change or the neighbor with an old grudge is getting more aggressive.

All these things happen slowly, not all at once. I think everyone knows the story of the frog in the pot of water. You turn up the temperature very slowly and the frog doesn't notice. I think we need to become much more aware of a change in the temperature. We need to pay better attention. In my parents' generation, that something like the Holocaust could happen was unimaginable. But today we know exactly what is possible, even if it only begins with slogans and statements in front of small crowds in a beer hall or posts on social media.

◦—◦

When I speak and tell my story, people ask me many things, but two questions come up every single time. The two questions are: "How did you survive?" and "Can the Holocaust happen again?" As to how I survived, my honest answer is that I do not really know. Luck, I guess, and my mother working hard and probably my basic determination to cling to life no matter what, which I still do.

As to the second question about whether the Holocaust can happen again, I think people are looking at it the wrong way. This is not like a Hollywood movie. Of course the Holocaust could not happen again exactly as it did.

The question really should be: Did we learn from the Holocaust? The answer is, I am sorry to say, not yet. But there is still time. And there is always hope. But we need more than hope; we need to educate ourselves and take action.

◦—◦

I shaved and combed my hair and wore my nicest white shirt and my special pendant that says GOOD LUCK ALONG THE WAY in Hebrew because I was going to the home of the EU ambassador to Israel. It was Yom HaShoah in 2022.

I had met ambassadors before, but this was a small gathering in the ambassador's home, and I would be able to meet each ambassador personally, so of course I was a bit nervous!

I was introduced by the Czech ambassador to Israel, and before long, I was sharing my story. Everyone listened very politely and asked a lot of good questions. I felt that I did a good job in such an intimate setting with such important dignitaries. Afterward, everybody was served coffee and tea and we all went outside for a big picture together. It took some time to get everybody arranged nicely in that photograph, which I still have.

To my great delight, the Rwandan ambassador to Israel, James Gatera, introduced himself and expressed his respect very kindly. He invited me to the Rwandan embassy to learn more about what the Rwandan people had gone through.

Not too long afterward, I went. The embassy was not big, but inside it was decorated with beautiful Rwandan baskets and art and pictures of the country, including the famous gorillas. The ambassador showed us around and then invited us to ask questions about the Rwandan genocide that occurred in 1994. I learned that the Hutus and the Tutsis, two tribes living for many years in this beautiful Central/East African country, played different roles in society and the economy of the land. Mostly, everyone got along, but militias set them against each other using propaganda mostly broadcast on the radio. After a while, the differences between these two tribes were inflamed to the point of terrible atrocity.

Between 500,000 and 800,000 Rwandans were murdered in this terrible war. Innocent people suffered, lost their loved ones, and died. It was butchery.

After my visit with the ambassador, I wanted to learn more about this terrible time, so Julie got me a book on Kindle called

We Wish to Inform You That Tomorrow We Will Be Killed with Our Families: Stories from Rwanda. It was written by Philip Gourevitch. Let me tell you, that book opened my eyes to a very complicated situation that had things in common with the Holocaust: opportunism, grudges, paranoia, intolerance, a lot of propaganda, and terrible brutality, all unleashed by ordinary people on ordinary people.

•◆•

"When we look at Auschwitz we see the end of the process. It's important to remember that the Holocaust actually did not start from gas chambers. This hatred gradually developed from words, stereotypes & prejudice through legal exclusion, dehumanisation & escalating violence."

This was posted on Twitter by the Auschwitz Memorial Museum in 2018, and I think this concept is so important to understand.

When most people think about the perpetrators of the Holocaust, they think of Nazis in their SS uniforms, like something from a movie or a black-and-white photo. But let me tell you something, there were many more guilty parties and they were not in a uniform at all. There were millions of enablers and they were, for the most part, ordinary people just like me and you.

There were people in the military and bureaucrats at the banks and factory bosses who saw the Nazis as an opportunity for advancing their careers and making immense profits. And there were brutes and thugs and criminals looking for any excuse to be violent, who were happy to beat Jews and others in the streets. There were university professors who wanted to enjoy favor, and socialites who wanted to be associated with whomever was in power because it brought them more status. There were people afraid to say anything, to go against the tide because they might lose their friends, jobs, or social status.

In other words, many people got caught up in a tide of Nazi hate because they wanted status, profit, and security more than they cared about the lives of those less fortunate than themselves. Or because they were glad the spotlight was on somebody else, not them. When I think about this today, I feel disgust and rage because millions of lives were lost for social status and more profits at the factory.

When things really got terrible, when people were being dragged away from their homes and put on trains, when people were being shot in front of ditches, many who supported the Nazis may have felt some fear or regret. But by then, it was too late. The Nazis were in power and nobody was safe. Before it got to that point, there were many opportunities to speak out and stand up for the principles of humanity. So many ordinary Germans could have and should have rejected the temptation of careers, status, brandy, and cigars. But that's not what they did. To be honest, I cannot forgive them for this.

Then and now, you have to be brave and principled. You have to be wary of self-interest. You have to be very aware of which influencers—whether they are politicians, intellectuals, teachers, social media influencers, or TV personalities and actors—you respect and why.

Question everything. Look deeper. Pay attention. Be discerning and check in on your own emotions. If you feel a strong emotion—ask where it is coming from. You have to start with yourself.

·◆·

There are always people out there who want power, money, influence, and attention. That's not new. But we ordinary people must be courageous and go against the tide, even if that means less money or a smaller house or fewer friends. These are not your friends and this is not a job promotion that you will feel good about in the future, because you got it off the suffering of others so you would be popular and accepted.

The fact is, I believe that the Holocaust was made possible by self-interest, greed, and ignorance. And I am afraid to say that these aspects of the human species are more or less unchanged. When people say "never again," they think of the most outspoken racist, antisemitic people, but really they should take a look at themselves and their friends. What would you do for a better life? What would you not do? How far would you go to improve your life? Who will lose out? Who will suffer?

We can make things better today and in the future if we value understanding the past. The Holocaust was less than a hundred years ago, but a shocking number of people all over the world know very little about it, and if they know anything, they see the Holocaust as an event that stands alone, totally apart from everything else. And in many terrible ways the Holocaust was totally unique, but if you don't understand what caused it to happen, never mind what actually happened, then you can't also fully understand everything that followed—even to this day.

When you study history, you can recognize patterns. If you don't like to read regular books, you can read graphic editions of books like *On Tyranny* by Timothy Snyder. That book made it very easy for me to get at least some understanding of the patterns and behaviors that people like Hitler, Mussolini, Stalin, Mao, and others have in common with one another.

Yuval Noah Harari is an Israeli writer I have been watching speak on YouTube quite a bit lately. He wrote a book about human history. Harari looks at history from a distance, and he explains how things flow from one to another. He explained how we humans grew and grew and eventually got into conflict with one another over land and resources. But what I really like is that he points out the patterns that exist in history. I think Harari is a very smart person worth listening to because if we see the patterns and recognize them, we can think harder about the possible results of our choices—good or bad.

I believe, with all my heart, that if we humans can turn salt water into fresh water and invent robots and send them to Mars, then we can also find solutions for problems that we have here on earth, especially because we created the problems ourselves. If humans created these problems, there's a good reason to believe we can also solve them.

•◆•

I think too many people today think too much about their own lives and what affects them much more than they think about the welfare of their neighbors and community. I believe that many of our problems in the world today could be addressed by thinking of not just our own countries, societies, and ourselves, but also all of us, living together on this earth.

Not putting yourself first is very natural to me because I lived the kibbutz life for fifteen years and then I raised five children, which is like a mini kibbutz. On a kibbutz, everything is done cooperatively. Everything is shared. There is a community dining hall where meals are taken together and a community laundry center where you drop off your clothes. Everybody works for the kibbutz to help it prosper for everyone. Everybody works hard. Nobody is above anybody else.

Eventually, I left kibbutz life behind because my beloved Susan was an American, and she and I together wanted to have more individual say over our lives. But that time in my life, of being a kibbutznik, was extremely important to me. The lessons of cooperative living never left me. This sometimes drives Julie crazy because she can't understand why everything has to be a discussion! But I stick to my ways because I think they are important.

I still have children, grandchildren, and even great-grandchildren who live on a kibbutz in the Jezreel Valley and I see them often. Everybody knows everybody else on a kibbutz, and families live there for generations. Sometimes in America and other places, neighbors don't always know each other. But on a kibbutz, it is one big family. This is just one of the reasons the brutal massacre on October 7 was so devastating for those communities and for all Israel because so many Israelis have friends and family who live on a kibbutz.

•–•

Today, we're all in the same boat and I think lots of things make that clear, for example, climate change. Nobody can escape the effects of the weather and the climate. Even though climate change is very troubling to me, one good thing, if you can say that, is that I hope it makes people realize that with all these borders and different governments and different cultures, we are all sharing the same place.

Sadly, hatred and antisemitism are among us again today. The fact is, antisemitism today is as high as it was in the 1930s, before the Holocaust. We have to stand up against it with all our hearts and souls. Antisemitism is not only a Jewish problem; it's a problem for all of us. People who are different are usually the canaries in the coal mine.

You don't have to be different to speak out against hate. You don't have to go to a fancy university to know history. I did not graduate from high school, but I know my history. You don't have to live on a kibbutz to be more connected to and caring about your family, friends, and community. You don't have to be an ambassador or diplomat to know that relationships between different kinds of people are important to care for and cultivate. We humans—all of us—need each other in all our diversity. We must embrace tolerance and understanding if we are to continue sharing this wondrous earth together. We must keep aware and look sharp because there are some people who wish we didn't stick together!

10

FAKE NEWS IS OLD NEWS

Gidon at Theresienstadt in 2023.

"**Y**OU'RE GOING TO A NICE PLACE." THAT'S WHAT THE GUARDS said.

I remember the truck that came to the entrance of the Dresden barracks. Some other children and I were in the courtyard, and the guards told us to get into the truck. Of course we were scared because we didn't know what that meant. But we got in the truck. We didn't have too much of a choice and by then we had learned to do as we were told and do it quickly because it was not unusual to get a kick or a slap.

A few minutes later, we were in the center of the camp and there was a playground that we had never seen before. It had sand and a slide, a merry-go-round, some swings, and things to climb on. The guards ordered us to get off the truck and to go play. We did as we were told. I remember being confused. This was something very strange. I didn't understand what was going on.

Then we saw in the distance, maybe a hundred yards away, some German officers and people with Red Cross armbands taking pictures of us, *flash flash flash*. They seemed very interested in what we were doing.

We did what children do in a playground, even though we knew people were watching us. We were always being watched in one way or another. I do recall a strange feeling, though. I didn't know who the people were who were taking our pictures or why they were doing it.

After a little while, I don't remember exactly how long, the people seemed to fade away and the cameras stopped flashing. Suddenly, we kids were herded back into the truck by the German officers and taken right back to our barracks without any explanation.

On a "normal" day, we kids mostly hunted for food and tried to avoid getting hit by the guards. Why did the Nazis take us to a playground? We never knew a playground was there at all. For many years, I did not know whether this was a real memory or some kind of a dream.

·—·

During World War II, more than forty-four thousand Nazi concentration camps were scattered across Europe. Almost all of them were forced labor camps where prisoners manufactured the munitions and equipment the Nazis needed to keep the war going.

The Nazis were very efficient. They wanted to work their prisoners until they could no longer work, and then they murdered them so they didn't have to feed them. If you couldn't work, you were killed right away. That is why so many old people and children were selected for death immediately.

Every camp had a purpose. There were POW camps. There were camps, like Dachau, that were for political prisoners. Ravensbrück was a camp in Germany that was only for women. Majdanek, Chelmno, Treblinka, Belzec, and Sobibor were camps for killing. Auschwitz-Birkenau was a death camp that also had forced labor and many subcamps surrounding it. In Flossenburg, the slave laborers got rock from a quarry that was sent to Berlin to make Nazi statues and buildings.

Theresienstadt also had a purpose. It was a propaganda tool for the Nazis. The Nazis even called Theresienstadt "the model ghetto." The camp was an elaborate lie to the Czech Jews, to the Jews in general, and to the whole world. I guess you could say that I was lucky to be there because the purpose of the camp was not for killing but for propaganda and to serve as a transit camp. I don't feel so lucky.

In the first period, when Theresienstadt was set up, the Nazis told my father, grandfather, and the other men that they would be employed to help ready Theresienstadt for the "resettled" Jews who were coming. The Nazis told the old people that they were going to a spa for elderly people and that it would be very nice in Theresienstadt. The Nazis sent members of the Jewish intelligentsia of Prague to Theresienstadt because they knew that if people like them, many of them famous, educated, and respected, just disappeared, then other people would begin to wonder. They had an explanation. These people, who all just so happened to be Jews, were simply being "resettled." Simple as that. And people believed them.

The truth is that Theresienstadt was a cover. The Nazis didn't want the Czech Jews to panic and try to flee. They wanted them to cooperate so they could gather them all in one place, force them to work, and then deport them to the death camps.

The "Model Ghetto" also allowed the Nazis to say to other countries, "Here. Take a look. Look how well these Jews live. They can shop, they can buy food, clothing." They could say, "See for yourself, we are not harming Jews, we are just 'resettling' them."

I feel so very angry about this, even today. I don't know which makes me more angry, the lies of the Nazis or that people chose to believe those lies. All you had to do was look a little bit more closely at Theresienstadt to see it was all a deception.

•◆•

For a long time, this strange memory of being taken to a playground was like other fragments of memories I have from my time in Theresienstadt. It didn't make sense, so I wasn't sure if it really happened or not. I questioned my memory. It was only later I discovered it was true.

The Third Reich depended on ball bearings and other military supplies that came to them from Sweden and Denmark. So when the Danish Red Cross asked to inspect Theresienstadt because over four hundred Danish Jews had been deported there, the Nazis more or less had to allow the visit. But they stalled for as long as possible so they would have time to prepare. And prepare they did.

Many months before the visit, the Nazis ordered a "beautification" to commence. They made prisoners paint, plaster, and even pave some streets. They had them plant over one thousand rosebushes and install the fake playground that I remember. They set up phony clothing, grocery, and repair stores. They even printed fake paper money. They put up signs pointing to nonexistent schools, swimming pools, and cafés. They renamed the streets regular names instead of the military letters and numbers they had used before.

On June 23, 1944, a delegation of the Danish Red Cross, the Danish foreign minister, and the International Red Cross arrived. High-ranking Nazi functionaries were also there. These were the people taking pictures of us kids.

The Nazis made some prisoners in Theresienstadt dress up like policemen and introduced the delegation to the "mayor" of Theresienstadt, who was really another prisoner, Council Elder Paul Eppstein. They made Eppstein show the visitors papers showing fake statistics about Theresienstadt that said everyone was eating well and was healthy. People who were disabled or sick were forbidden to leave their rooms on that day. The Nazis told the prisoners to smile and pretend they were shopping for things and hand over the fake money at the fake stores. The clothing at the "clothing store" had actually belonged to the prisoners in the first place.

They even let us prisoners have a big soccer match with teams and people cheering. A performance of the children's opera *Brundibár* was held for the visitors to see.

The people in the Danish Red Cross delegation who spent the day in Theresienstadt were duped. The same way they dumped us kids on the playground and told us to play, the Nazis led the delegation around and said, "Here. Look at this. And only this." The delegation saw exactly what the Nazis wanted them to. A Jewish village with shops and a mayor, sports, and culture. None of it was real.

The delegation did not know the truth. They did not know and of course the Nazis did not tell them that to make the camp less crowded during their visit, they had gathered up and sent 7,500 prisoners to the east, where those poor souls surely met their deaths.

After that visit, the Nazis decided to make use of all the fake things they had set up and made a propaganda film. They did not want to miss the opportunity for more lies.

The film was called *The Führer Gives a City to the Jews* and was directed by one of the prisoners of Theresienstadt. I saw part of this film at the Theresienstadt museum during my last visit there. Watching the faces in the film, some of them smiling, some of them looking as if they want to cry, and knowing that they were all murdered anyway fills me with fury. I have looked and looked to see if I am in this film or in the photos the Red Cross took, but I can't see myself.

Two weeks after the film was done, the director and all the people who had appeared in the film were sent to Auschwitz.

·•·

Fake news is nothing new. In fact, the Germans, as far back as WWI, even had a name for it: *Lügenpresse*, which means "lying press." Hitler and his cronies used this expression a lot. If news came out that they couldn't deny, they would say it was "the lying press"—that it was fake news, in other words. But *lügenpresse* could be used in favor of the Nazis too. They put out their own fake news and persuaded people that what they said was true. After a while, people didn't know what was true and what was false.

The same thing is happening today, using different technology and techniques that are a great deal more sophisticated. So much so, that we can hardly tell when news is news, if news is fake, or if news is just entertainment and not real at all.

The Nazis used the radio to broadcast their messages as much as possible. Joseph Goebbels was the minister of propaganda for the Nazis, and you could almost say he was a genius. An evil genius. He even said: "Propaganda should be popular, not intellectually pleasing. It is not the task of propaganda to discover intellectual truths."

Goebbels negotiated the creation of a special radio that was much cheaper so that more Germans could afford one to listen to the propaganda of the Nazis. This was in 1933, before the war started, so you can see that this propaganda went on for some time.

In Nazi Germany, Germans would see films or read pamphlets or newspaper articles that said that the Jews were cheating them and making Germany a bad place and saying all sorts of things that made Germans feel angry and scared. Or they saw things that showed how wonderful Germans were and how great "Aryans" were and how proud German culture was. And that made them feel good. But then they saw the other stuff and that made them feel angry and scared, so it was a lot of manipulation.

Before the Holocaust and WWII, Germans were in a vulnerable state. They suffered a humiliating loss in the First World War and their economy was terrible. There was confusion and anger. They needed to find a reason for why they had lost and they had to find a way to overcome what had happened. Antisemitism was something that already existed all over Europe and at that time, somewhat like today, it wasn't something people kept to themselves. But it was waiting to be unleashed, to be given permission. And that's what the Nazis did. They took advantage of all these existing circumstances.

I have tried to learn about and understand the manipulation and brainwashing that propaganda and fake news are capable of. I don't think in Germany, in the 1930s, anyone would have believed what direction everything was headed. It's true that many people just plain hated the Jews, so they weren't really brainwashed, they were just encouraged to hate Jews more. But others allowed themselves to be manipulated because they didn't bother to pay closer attention and ask questions.

Today I see this happening again, not only in one place like Germany but all over the world, and it's even being fueled and encouraged. I must admit I find it shocking and it angers me how many people are falling for this manipulation because, today, we know exactly what happened in the past. Now there is no excuse. This is why what happened in the wake of October 7 is deeply distressing to me. Because we definitely know better.

·•·

On October 7, 2023, Hamas terrorists came into Israel from Gaza and committed unspeakable atrocities on Israeli civilians. Everyone in Israel was shocked and upset, including me and Julie. It was the worst, most barbaric attack on us Jews since the Holocaust.

The same day, videos began flooding in on the television news and social media. Videos of terrible things. There were things done during that horrific day that I am very sorry that I saw and that I will never, ever forget. Things much more terrible than anything I ever saw in the Holocaust.

Not long after, some people on social media starting saying that the October 7 massacre never took place. These terrible events had just happened—the terrorists actually filmed themselves committing their atrocities. How could people deny what happened?

It was upsetting to both Julie and me that many of the same young people who had been following my Holocaust education videos were so quickly and easily influenced by and uncritical of what they were hearing and seeing in the media and on social media about October 7. How could this be? This was exactly what we had been trying to teach; not just the history of the Holocaust and not just parts of my story, but we tried to show how groups of people who did not think critically were in danger of being manipulated.

When so many young people, without thinking carefully and critically, begin echoing the thoughts, feelings, and ideas of others, we have to watch out. I'm very sad and very disappointed to see what is happening today, but I still believe we can do better.

For example, I found out about "media literacy," which is something that teaches people how to be more aware of how media influences their opinions, thoughts, and even their lives. There are many organizations that support and teach media literacy, and they can help people learn what to watch out for and notice. I encourage anyone reading this book to invest some of their time into learning about media literacy. We simply must learn how to understand the strong influence that media and social media have on our lives. We cannot just echo the thoughts and ideas of others; we must question, all the time.

One little media-literacy trick that I learned is that if a social media post makes you angry—stop and think about that. Ask yourself who made what you just saw. Ask why they said or posted what they did. Ask what their agenda might be.

And the opposite is also important. If you see a social media post or some news report or article that makes you feel happy and good, you should ask the same questions.

•→•

Today the internet has opened up the world to much more scrutiny but also wields a great deal of influence. This makes us more susceptible today than ever.

Everyone, from politicians to supermarket chains to car salesmen, will always want to influence us. They want us to buy their products or ideas. None of this has changed.

But we have changed. We are wiser now. The fact is, eighty or more years ago, people were not aware that their emotions were susceptible to manipulation. But people today are aware on one level or another that the media can and does affect our emotions, opinions, and even our actions—for better or worse.

We must truly be alert and on guard at all times. Whether you agree or disagree with a position, ask yourself, Who is presenting this opinion or information? Who are they trying to influence and what will they gain? Sometimes it might just be a social media influencer who is gaining "likes" or popularity. In other cases, it might be a political group trying to influence voters and political outcomes.

I am lucky to have survived a time when a few very bad people influenced the minds of millions of others, which caused unimaginable cruelty and suffering to take place.

I am sorry to say that we are still very much vulnerable to these kinds of influences today. That said, I do have hope that believing in ourselves, using our common sense, thinking critically, and looking clearly at our world and its challenges will, in the end, prevail.

11

LEARNING TO BELIEVE IN MYSELF

Gidon protesting in Tel Aviv.

Gidon speaking at the EJA conference in Prague in 2023.

MY KIDS SHOW ABUNDANT LOVE AND AFFECTION FOR ME AND for each other and this really warms my heart. As different in character as they are one from the other, they share a very strong bond and give each other a great deal of care, love, and respect. When they are gathered together, my kids discuss their lives, jobs, and experiences and the doings of their own children, my grandchildren. And, of course, they also tease each other and tell many stories of growing up.

If you were there, you might overhear my kids say, "Do you remember when Dad did this?" or "Remember when Mom did that?" or "Remember that time Dad's briefcase almost got blown up?"

•-•·

We were just about ten minutes away from the pizza place where my family and I had stopped for lunch in Haifa when I realized that I was going to be fired from one of the best jobs I'd ever had. What an idiot, I kept telling myself over and over. Idiot, idiot!

I was working for a fine gold and jewelry importer, exporter, and designer. I was the person who did all the import and export paperwork for the company and the calculation of the wages for about a dozen goldsmiths. I had my own office and I truly enjoyed this job. It was full of challenges and responsibilities, and I learned a tremendous lot about jewelry and the workings of the high-end gold business. I would never have imagined myself with such a job!

One day, my boss needed to get a package with a number of 18 carat gold bracelets to Switzerland very urgently. Usually, he would put a package like that in the mail, insured, of course, and send it to Ben Gurion Airport, and from there it would be sent on its way. But there had been a mistake of some kind and the package needed to be hand-delivered to the airport. My boss was very much in a hurry. He was, as we would say in Yiddish, "on *shpilkes*" about it. When he took me aside and asked me to make the delivery, I said, in essence, *"Hineni!"* Mistake number one.

Hineni is a special word that has a lot of meaning to me. Translated from Hebrew, it means something like "Here I am, I am ready." It is what Abraham said to God when God first spoke to him. It is what Moses said to God when God told him to go up the mountain to receive the Ten Commandments.

I think in today's way of speaking, *hineni* might mean something like "showing up," and I have always endeavored to do just that. But this was one day when I really wish I hadn't!

I wanted to be a good employee and I didn't want to disappoint my boss. I had all the export paperwork filled out and everything was in order—what could go wrong? I put the three parcels into a sturdy briefcase to make them easier to carry. Mistake number two.

Me being me, I decided to make a day of it and bring Sue and the kids along so we could stop in Tel Aviv to visit with Sue's parents, Monty and Margie, and have some supper. That way the kids could visit with their grandparents and the day would be good and fun for all of us.

We were all in a good mood when we left and as we were passing near Haifa, we remembered that our favorite pizza place wasn't too far off. My family loved pizza, so being a bit hungry, Sue and I thought, Why not? We stopped for pizza with the kids. Mistake number three.

I don't remember what kind of pizza we ordered that day, probably pepperoni because that's my favorite, but I do remember that we were all in jolly high spirits by the time we finished our lunch. We walked back to our car, buckled everybody up again, and continued driving south toward Tel Aviv. A few minutes later, Sue looked around the car and said, "Gidon, where is your briefcase?"

·◆·

I never thought of myself as a very clever person. After I was liberated, I was happy to finally be able to go to school, but I was very much behind the other kids and that was clear to me and everyone else. Though I could read and write a little, I had never learned arithmetic, history, or geography, and this was very much a handicap. Not only that, after the Nazi regime occupied Czechoslovakia, they took over the education of the children. I told you before about Nazi propaganda. That also applied to what kids living under Nazi occupation learned in schools. The fact is, the Nazis invested a lot of energy into indoctrinating kids. No wonder that kid called me a "stupid Jew." I had to hold my own and I did because there was no other choice, but I do think that this period left me with many insecurities.

When it came time to go to high school in Toronto, I decided to go to a high school that specialized in teaching a trade rather than preparing young people for university. I told myself that it was because I needed to learn a trade to fulfill my dream of living on a kibbutz and being a hard worker. But when I look back, to tell you the truth, I think there was a little bit more to it. I think there was a part of me that doubted my ability to do well at a school that prepared people for higher education.

At Central Technical School, I studied motor mechanics about ten hours a week, in addition to my regular school studies. During our classes, we had to wear either a motor mechanic's outfit or at least some sort of overcoat. I would have liked to wear the motor mechanic uniforms they had, but they were too big for me.

I was a very serious student and my instructors liked me. During these studies, I learned all about the combustion engine and the principles of how it works and I loved it. A car has different parts and they all have to work together. I learned a lot about carburetors, which was the part of the engine that mixed air and gasoline at a certain ratio and then moved it to the engine, where it essentially exploded and made our cars go forward. Doing repairs on an engine is a little bit like a doctor doing surgery; you have to be very precise.

Of course, over the years, as with everything, motor mechanics, cars, engines, and electronics have changed so much that I hardly understand how today's cars work, especially those running on electricity. But believe it or not, I still drive, and I still love cars!

Unfortunately, I didn't finish high school. I dropped out three months before I would have graduated. I wanted badly to work, earn money, and be independent from my mother. This was a decision that I did come to regret.

•-•-•

During one of my periods of living in Canada when my kids were small, unemployment was very high and jobs were few and far between. I couldn't find a job, and this affected my self-esteem.

I was forty-six years old, a father, and the breadwinner, but I wasn't putting bread on the table. Luckily, Susan was teaching

English to new immigrants, but with such a large family, we could not live on one income alone.

All my life, work was my anchor, yet here I was, out of work and with a family to support. It really made me doubt myself and my choices, but I was determined to find a job and I was not afraid to work hard.

In the morning when the newspapers came out, I went to buy the *Toronto Daily Star* and the *Globe and Mail*. I came back home, made myself a cup of tea, looked through the Help Wanted sections, and circled possibilities.

One day I saw an advertisement for a two-week training program to learn to be a vacuum cleaner salesman. I had a friendly personality and I liked talking to people, so why not? Maybe I could succeed.

I enrolled in the program and I actually enjoyed it. It was fun! About fifteen other people were in the training program with me. First, the trainers taught us about the vacuum cleaner itself, how it worked, how wonderful it was, and all the things it could do. They put some dirt on the carpet and showed us how easily this vacuum cleaner sucked it right up and into the canister. They showed us how to take apart and clean the machine and what to do if it got blocked. Being mechanically minded, this I enjoyed.

Then they taught us some of the techniques of being a good salesman. We were taught how to approach, how to convince, how to be complimentary and friendly. All this seemed very simple and natural to me. I felt that I would be a big success!

After the training was over, the vacuum company would call us salespeople and say, "Okay, go to Palmerston Avenue 21, third floor, apartment 28, Mrs. Diamond." So, I would put on some nice clothes, shave, brush my hair, take my demonstrator vacuum, and go to the address. I would knock on the door, introduce myself, and demonstrate how well the vacuum worked. I would even ask Mrs. So-and-So if I could wet her hair to show her how the machine could dry hair, but for some reason the ladies always declined!

I thought this job had a lot of potential because it was a good vacuum cleaner and I am a friendly and warm person. But try as I might—and I did try hard for over two months—I sold only one vacuum machine, and that was to my mother.

Not long after that, I saw an advertisement in the newspaper for a course to learn computer programming. This was something different for me because I really didn't know anything about computers. But I decided to give it a shot.

I went to the course and quickly noticed that I was about twice the age of the other students. Here I was, out of a job, in my midforties, and the other students were in their twenties. I felt very self-conscious. The other students in the program acted differently, they dressed differently, and I guess they didn't have several kids at home! They also seemed to speak their own language, or so it seemed to me, using words and lingo that I did not understand about computers and programming. Seeing how quickly the others caught on to our computer-programming lessons, I felt lost and inadequate. After only a few sessions, I quit the class.

Today I realize that I was putting too much emphasis on my self-esteem because of this or that job and my ability to earn money for my family. But it is only human to need small victories and encouragement in our lives. We need to know that success is possible. Had I been able to sell even a handful of vacuum cleaners, I might have stuck with it. Had even one or two people in the computer-programming class been my age or also struggled, I might have stuck with that too.

Discouragement when nothing seems to work out is a terrible feeling. We begin to think we will never succeed. We look at other people around us and think that they are better than us because they are younger or older, more educated, successful, or even better looking.

The fact is that it is very human to feel insecure at times, but it is important not to allow that discouragement to overcome us. Everybody has gifts, talents, and abilities at every age and stage of our lives. We can't compare ourselves to other people because everybody is different.

We only discover what our abilities are by experimenting and trying—and, yes, sometimes failing. This is part of life. Just keep showing up. Don't be too afraid of failure—you might just learn something and even have a good story to tell in the end.

—◆—

Realizing that I had left a briefcase with at least $50,000 worth of gold jewelry in it in a pizza parlor, I should have just kept on driving. I was going to lose my job, there was nothing I could do. Yet, I couldn't give up so easily. Me being me, I made a split-second decision and made a U-turn so fast, the kids slid all the way to one side of the car. They were shocked. They said, "Dad, be careful!" I sped back to the pizza place, hoping that the briefcase was where I left it.

But a hundred yards from the pizza place, I had to slam on my brakes. The entire road was blocked and there were policemen and flashing lights everywhere. They were closing down every street that led to the pizza parlor. There was no way to get past that many policemen. I didn't know what to do. But I couldn't give up.

My kids can tell you how, to their shock, seeing a wall of policemen blocking the street, their father stopped the car and ran straight toward the police waving his arms like a wild man.

The sappers already had my briefcase surrounded and were ready to blow it up! With the kids and Susan in the car watching with their eyes wide, I did some fast talking. Even though I knew that I would be fired when my boss found out what had happened, I still felt responsible to save that jewelry from being blown up. I showed the police my paperwork, which had the name of the company I was working for on it. I just knew they would call my boss and check. But somehow—they didn't. I guess they could see how desperate I was and how much I needed to save my job. Suddenly, everybody stood back from my briefcase at quite a distance and let me through.

Carefully, I inched forward and slowly opened the briefcase to show them what was inside.

In the end, the police gave me back the briefcase, all in one piece, and I kept my job because I never told my boss what happened!

•-•-•

Conquering self-doubt and fear of failure is a lifelong process that never ends. I struggled with self-doubt recently, on my last birthday, when I turned eighty-nine.

You see, each year on my birthday, Julie likes to surprise me with a new adventure, each different from the last and each one wonderful. For my most recent birthday, she decided to surprise me with a weekend in the desert followed by a visit to a race car track!

I couldn't believe it. I have been driving for over seventy-four years, but I have never driven a race car. I was excited but nervous when we got to the race track. I did not know what it would be like or whether I could handle a race car at my age. I didn't want to look foolish.

My race car instructor was a champion driver and the first thing he did was open the hood of the car and we looked at the engine together. You can only imagine how fascinating this was for me, having studied combustion engines so long ago. My instructor explained about the cylinders of the car, what kind of fuel it used, and how the engine worked. He went over the basics of how to get the car around the track safely at very high speeds and how to take corners and use the centrifugal force. He told me that precision and control were the two most important things when driving a car like this. I began to have doubts. Precision and control are not things I am so sure about at my age. I had never driven such a fast car and I couldn't remember the last time I drove a stick shift. I thought, Gidon Lev, is this a good idea? So I looked around at the track, at my instructor, at the other cars whizzing by, and I said to myself, Why not? *Hineni!* Jump right in, Gidon Lev!

I got into that red race car and took right off. We went around the track several times, going faster each time as I got more used to the workings of the car. I surprised myself and I think I shocked my instructor! Later I found out that the instructor did not have another pair of brakes, so he must have said *hineni* before we started and *shehechiyanu* when we were done!

⋅•⋅

One day when I was wandering around Jerusalem enjoying the sights while Julie was having lunch with a friend she hadn't seen in some time, I happened upon a small shop filled with beautiful jewelry and candlesticks and all manner of beautifully crafted silver. I struck up a conversation with the silversmith, who was from Yemen, and he showed me his fine work. Then I saw a beautiful silver ring that I wanted Julie to have.

I asked the silversmith to engrave a message on the ring, something that Julie would remember forever and that would remind her of me. I thought about it for a long while and then came to a decision. The silversmith engraved one word: *Hineni.*

12

LIVING HEART AND SOUL

(*Left to right*) Gidon's children: Maya, Hadasa, Asher, Elisha, Gidon (*seated*), Yanai (*seated, holding his son Eshel*), and Shaya (*seated*) in 1994.

O N OCTOBER 10, 2020, SOMETHING VERY SPECIAL HAPPENED in the Lev family. My baby—that is, my youngest son, Asher—became a father for the first time. This birth was a very special one because the midwife who was supposed to deliver the baby did not arrive on time and Asher had to deliver his little son, Moshé, himself. I was so amazed and proud of him.

Asher is the only one of my children at whose delivery I was allowed to be present. I was right there, holding Susan's hand and encouraging her. I was right there to greet Asher on his first day of life. And so it was for Asher and his son, Moshé Lev!

•➤•

Of course I wanted to get on a plane and go to Brussels to congratulate Asher and Irina and to greet my youngest grandchild, but it was not to be. I felt cheated, sad, and angry all in one big lump.

All this was happening during the COVID pandemic. It was a terrible, frightening, and at times heartbreaking time for millions of people all over the world, including me. I recall very clearly that it was a confusing and scary time. Nobody knew what was going on, what the dangers were, and how to deal with this terrible virus—people were dying and it was frightening to watch the television news at night.

Julie was probably more scared than me during this time. She was so afraid I would get sick. She wouldn't let me go into the grocery store with her. She put on her mask and went in herself while I waited in the car. She protected me to the hilt.

When the stores ran out of the disinfectant sprays, Julie went to work in the kitchen and made a special concoction of lavender oil and rubbing alcohol that we used to wipe things down so that we would hopefully not get sick with this terrible virus.

During those times, the streets were deserted and an eerie quietness enveloped not just our immediate neighborhood but also the entire city and even country. This was happening all over the world. Stores were closed and the streets were unusually empty and quiet with so few cars. Airports and bus stations were closed down, as were movie theaters and restaurants. It was truly a very unusual and trying time, something that I had never experienced before in my life.

One of the worst parts of it, of course, was that people could not gather in groups, with their families or friends. Many of us felt isolated and lonely a good part of the time. Julie and I had each other, but of course we missed being around others too.

•◆•

In April, one of the most important of our holiday celebrations, Passover, arrived once more. But during the pandemic, the question for all of us was how could we celebrate and yet not be together? How could we share the joy of celebrating freedom, emancipation, and the coming of the spring all in our separate homes?

Passover in my family has always been a festive affair. We enjoy the Passover seder with the wonderful food and rituals, drinking the cups of wine and retelling the story of the flight of our people from Egypt thousands of years ago. Much thought and preparation always goes into it and that gives the entire holiday a rewarding feeling for us. The entire Lev family takes part in it, children and adults, friends and family. We love it every year and everybody puts a lot of heart into it. In fact, our family name, Lev, means "heart" in Hebrew.

But, sadly, this Passover was held on Zoom. We tried our best, going through the motions, but the personal contact was missing. It was nowhere as lively or celebratory as usual. To me, the silver lining was that this made me realize and truly appreciate how wonderful our family celebrations and traditions usually are and how important it is to continue them.

◦—◦

Thank goodness, after some time, the COVID virus finally abated. Yet other challenges and problems took its place. These days, things are changing and happening at a furious pace and there is a lot of upheaval. Therefore, there is a tremendous lot of trepidation and anxiety all over the world. It feels like many of us have forgotten how to talk to each other, to reason through, argue, and maybe even solve at least some of our problems.

To me, there is simply no substitute for sitting in the same kitchen or around the dining table or in the living room and hearing, seeing, and feeling each other's thoughts and emotions, soul to soul, heart to heart, and, as we say in Hebrew, *panim el'panim*, or "face-to-face." It is an essential part of our humanity and somewhat of a lost art.

◦—◦

When the kids were growing up, Susan had a policy that none of us in the family should ever go to bed angry. So, when we argued, which of course we did, she would organize us in the living room to talk through it. It was, at times, very difficult. The kids, being angry or upset about something, would rather have slammed their bedroom door and listened to music. But Susan simply wouldn't allow that.

Our tribe was a big one, and we had to learn to work things out and to compromise. We had to learn how to express ourselves and to listen. Sometimes the hour grew late, and we got tired and were not making progress on resolving our differences. Susan would say, "So you are tired, you have got to go to school or work in the morning? Well, open up your heart!" We didn't always manage to make things better, but the rule in our home was that we had to try. We did not run away from difficult conversations or strong emotions, we made our way through them, together.

Once, after Susan and I had argued and gone to bed without making up, a big no-no in our family, I woke up the next morning to find a beautiful, colorful sign on our refrigerator. It said: LET'S MAKE THINGS BETTER. Susan must have stayed up for hours making it. To this very day, I still have it and I try to live by those words, even if I'm not sure how to make things better.

I will admit that, lately, even I, "Mr. Cheerful," do not feel as optimistic or hopeful as I usually do. Listening to the radio or watching the television news certainly does not help. Luckily, I have a friend named Elaine who lives just a few miles from Julie and me, in a village called Tzippori. Elaine and her late husband, Frank, have been our friends for the last forty-five years. Sadly, Frank passed away about a year ago. We all were very sad about it, but Elaine has managed to carry on a very vibrant and active life. I think that it is clear that because Elaine has always cultivated and kept up with many friends in her community and built such a loving family with Frank, she was better able to weather his departure and carry on living too.

I love going to Elaine's house because it's a sunny and cheerful home and she is always busy gardening and cooking and doing. Elaine is very welcoming, no matter when I come by. She simply hands me something to chop for dinner or puts a bowl of soup in front of me. Her front door is always open and she keeps the radio on so there is music in the house. It is always very relaxing there.

Elaine's garden is truly wild and natural, overflowing with thyme, mint, fruit trees, flowers, and even a small pond for the frogs. Believe me, those frogs do make themselves known, especially at night!

Julie and I go to see Elaine whenever we can. We usually bring something we made, bread or cake or even pickles or soup, and Elaine usually sends us home with fresh lemons from her tree or herbs from her garden. Sometimes when we visit, we talk about what is on the news and how we feel about politics and what the future might be. Other times we talk about growing herbs and how much sun they need or what books we are reading. Just being together, all of us, schmoozing as we peel oranges or eat soup is so relaxing, enriching, and nourishing for all our souls. I always return home feeling better and more whole and balanced.

•◆•

For me, there is no question that spending time with my friends and family is very important for my state of mind, happiness, and well-being. It's not always possible to spend time together in person, though. For example, my oldest friend, Paul Davidovitz, lives in New York. We have known each other since 1949—a very long time. We were only kids when we met. Because we live on different continents, it is very,

very rare that we can see each other in person. In fact, I can't remember the last time we did. But we do get on Zoom and catch up and I must admit that I enjoy that very much.

I am proud that Paul and I both have managed to continue our friendship for seventy-five years no matter how many miles (or differences!) are between us. Seventy-five years! Somehow, when we talk, we manage to pick up where we left off the last time. I find it very gratifying and even moving to keep such an important connection over so many years. We have both changed, and much time has gone by, but we still like each other just the same as we did when we first met.

•◆•

You can only imagine how excited I was when I was finally able to go to Brussels to meet my newest grandson, Moshé, the following year, on the occasion of his first birthday.

Moshé is such a delightful little boy, I can hardly talk about him without my eyes tearing up out of joy. Meeting him for the very first time was very emotional for me.

Together with Asher and Irina, we took Moshé in his stroller to a very special and large park in Brussels, where there were beautiful trees and meadows. Moshé was bundled up head to toe and his cheeks were pink as he did what babies do: look curiously at the trees and grass and the birds and even try to take a few steps before landing on his tuchus!

In the evenings, Asher cooked good food for us, and even with his bib on, Moshé managed to cover almost his entire body with the food meant to go in his mouth. We watched as

Moshé took his evening bath, enjoying the warm water and the bubbly soap, and then Irina sang him to sleep.

Moshé's birthday party was colorful and fun. It was a clown theme and Asher and Irina's friends and their children decorated their home with ribbons, streamers, and balloons. I ended up having a lovely Ping-Pong game with the balloons and little Moshé. Everybody put on costumes and funny wigs, including Julie and me both! Moshé looked around in wonder, and when he saw his birthday cake, he took his chubby little hands and tasted it right away.

Julie made a special gift for Moshé that she brought along with us to Brussels. She had crocheted a heart and then another one, a bit smaller. Before she closed up the small heart, she asked me to write a *bracha*—a blessing—for Moshé. This I did and then Julie put the blessing inside the little heart and put that heart inside the bigger heart. Then we wrapped the whole thing up and gave it to Moshé. He will just have to guess what my blessing is until, one day, he opens up his heart to find out!

When our wonderful and gratifying visit came to an end, we went to the airport to catch a flight to New York to visit with friends and family there. But it was not to be! At the airport, at the very last minute, we discovered that only those with American passports could enter the USA because of COVID restrictions. That meant that Julie could go but not me. I urged her to go ahead without me, but she just looked at me like I was crazy.

We were so disappointed, but we put our heads together with our friends and family to think of what to do. Hadasa was the one who came up with a great suggestion. Because trains did not have the same restrictions as airplanes, and because we had planned on traveling and visiting friends for a long time, why not take a train to Germany to visit some very, very special friends of mine? It was not what had been planned, it was very last minute, but I thought, Why not? And this we did.

So once more, we said our goodbyes to Brussels and we got on a train to Munich to visit with my dear friends Robert and Edel, whom I had met and befriended many years ago when they were visiting Israel. As our friendship developed, I learned that Edel's grandfather was in the Nazi Party during the war. He'd even had a big Nazi banner with a swastika on it on his house! I will admit that discovery was shocking to me, but I could also see and feel how painfully difficult it was for them to admit this to me, a Holocaust survivor.

The truth is, over time, Robert, Edel, and their daughter, Julia, and I learned a lot from each other about our different family histories and perspectives. It is heartwarming to me that both work very hard in Germany today to fight antisemitism and hatred of any kind.

Robert and Edel welcomed our unplanned visit with open arms. Edel cooked for us nonstop, and we enjoyed our meals in her cozy kitchen, which has a glass door overlooking a beautiful garden outside. Edel is a tremendous cook—just when you think you cannot eat another bite, out come German cakes, cookies, custards, and other delicacies.

Over the many meals during our visit, and the countless cups of coffee and wonderful desserts, we talked and caught up with each other for hours. Our conversations wandered all over the place, from Robert's profession as the commissioner against antisemitism for the Bavarian State to our train ride from Brussels to events of years past and more.

It might seem strange for someone with my past history to sit and talk with Germans, speaking German, so many years after such terrible events, yet I value this friendship because it proves that, with time, it is possible to build meaningful and caring connections that can help us heal the deep wounds of the past.

·—·

One day during the visit, everybody sort of disappeared, which I thought was strange. I was in the salon when up the stairs came an old man with his arms outstretched.

It was Michael Bergman! You may remember, Michael also survived Theresienstadt and I knew him after the war. I hadn't seen him since I was back in Karlovy Vary, seventy-three years ago!

The first moment Michael and I saw each other after so long was exhilarating. Robert, Edel, and Julie all reappeared smiling and clapping and crying a little.

My lucky star was really looking out for me on this last-minute trip to Germany. What it was like to see each other after all those years is hard to describe. Just imagine, when we last parted, we were about twelve years old. We had both survived the unthinkable. And now here we were, just two old guys, overjoyed to see each other once again.

During our visit, Michael and I spent time taking walks, one of which was around a big lake near his home. It was in the autumn and the trees were covered with red and gold leaves and it was a bit chilly. We could see our breath. As these two old guys strolled around the lake, our conversation meandered in all sorts of directions. It meant so much to me, since memory is fickle, that Michael is someone who can corroborate some of my earliest memories of being in the camp. In fact, it was Michael who reminded me of how we kids used to use sharp sticks to get at the rotten potatoes. I had forgotten all about that! He even reminded me of the time, after the war when we lived in the same old building, when my mother invited him to have lunch with us, and she served Czech dumplings called *knedlíky*, which at that time I abhorred. Michael reminded me that every time my mother looked aside, I would slip one of those dumplings stealthily into my pocket to be dumped into the garbage later. This was truly funny, since I did not remember this at all.

As we walked along, many deeper feelings and memories surfaced about how our lives were then and how they are now. There were kids playing near the lake, which reminded us of ourselves way back when, and Michael told me some of his favorite jokes. We were not in a hurry, we did not look at our phones, we just enjoyed the path and the trees and each other.

I don't know if I will ever see Michael again, but I will never forget how it felt to see him coming up the stairs of Robert and Edel's house or our walk around the lake, just two old guys, side by side, talking about the twists and turns of life. And it just so happens that one such twist and turn—me not being able to fly to New York—was what allowed me to experience a totally unexpected visit with an old, old friend, someone who just so happens to be the only other person in the world that I know shares the memories of surviving Theresienstadt.

•—•

I never in a million years would have imagined that I would reach the age I am today and that my life would have as many chapters as it has. The fact is, I am still here, writing new chapters in my life. I am open to new adventures, trying new things, and making new friends.

In my new community of Timrat, in northern Israel, I put myself out there by going to different events that are offered. A WhatsApp group shows what is going on, where, and at what time. It shows everything, from where you can go to pick up some fresh lemons to where you can attend special lectures and concerts and community activities for young and old. I have gone to several talks and concerts already.

At first, I felt a bit awkward because it seemed like everybody knew everybody else already, but I just smiled and was friendly and waited to see what it would be like. Recently, I went to a community event where everybody brought a wooden or plastic chair that could be painted, and we all gathered and painted colorful designs on them. We did this to honor and remember and send love to all those who have suffered and died in this terrible war between Israel and Hamas. I didn't exactly know what to expect, but Julie and I brought two chairs and we went. I painted two chairs in bright colors. On one I painted the word *Hope* and on the other I painted the word *Joy*.

Lo and behold, at that event I made a couple of new friends, including a wood sculptor. It turns out that Itzhak was in the same kibbutz movement that I was in, making him a real left-winger, so we two old guys have a lot in common!

I discovered that Itzhak doesn't live too far from me, so it is easy for me to go over to his house to see what he is up to, which is quite a lot. Itzhak is so impressive: He gets up at four or five in the morning, and he's no longer a young man, barely ten years younger than I am. Right now, he is making sculptured walking sticks for injured soldiers, each the exact right length and with the name of the person to receive it carved into it.

When I visit with Itzhak, we usually don't talk about what is going on in the world today. We don't really talk that much at all. We are just together. He is going through treatment for cancer and I very well know what that is like, so mostly I just keep quiet and watch him work carefully, being his creative self.

I am so inspired by his devotion to his craft and the care he puts into each walking stick. Not too long ago, Itzhak gave me a walking stick he made just for me. I know he worked hard on it and that means quite a bit to me.

Somehow, just quietly watching Itzhak work makes me feel good and calm. It takes my mind off the many worrisome things going on in this world. I think it's important for our hearts and souls to do things that make us feel good.

And when we don't feel so good, when we are worried or afraid, if we can share our feelings and our thoughts with others, it really does help because it reminds us that we are all in this crazy world together.

We humans manage to do all sorts of things, good and sometimes very bad, yet somehow, we are still here, living, creating, and doing. And, yes, also arguing and destroying and rebuilding all over again. As King David once said, "*Gam zeh y'avor*," which means "This too shall pass."

I sometimes wonder—what keeps us all going, over so many thousands of centuries, from good times to hard times and back again? The answer to the question is simple: We get through hard times together. Sometimes over bowls of soup or walks around a lake or being together on Zoom. Usually with tears, laughter, silly jokes, arguments, love, and whatever else comes our way. *Panim el'panim*, heart to heart, soul to soul.

13

THE HILLS AND VALLEYS

Gidon on Kibbutz Hazorea in 1959.

ONE YEAR FOR MY BIRTHDAY SURPRISE, JULIE ARRANGED FOR US to go up in a hot-air balloon over the Jezreel Valley. Let me tell you, the view from a thousand feet or more up in the sky, looking down over all this wonderful green earth, is quite extraordinary. I have spent years of my life down on the ground in this valley, plowing the fields and harvesting the hay, but I had never, ever seen the land from so high up in the sky. Everything seems so small and orderly, laid out in straight lines and clear patterns. Down on the ground, life is anything but orderly!

After almost an hour of peacefully drifting among the clouds in the blue skies above the Jezreel Valley, we began our descent. Watching the earth get closer and closer again, with everything slowly regaining its normal size and shape, we touched down, but it wasn't a totally smooth landing. Only a second or two later, as our huge balloon was beginning to deflate very slowly, a man ran up to us at top speed. He was shouting and angry and threatened to call the police!

It turned out, our hot-air balloon pilot had misjudged and we had landed in the farmer's field without his permission. The farmer was very worked up. We had not damaged any of his crops, but it was freshly plowed earth and I surely know how much work that involves.

Quickly, we all piled out and, together, helped take care of any damage we had done. Soon enough, the farmer calmed down and even laughed at such a crazy incident. When he found out it was my birthday, he said, "*Kol hakavod, ad mea ve esrim!*" This is a blessing said to older people, especially on their birthday, and it means something like "Much respect, may you live to a hundred and twenty!" I am not so sure I want to live that long, though. I think the important thing is *how* you live your years, not how *many* years you live.

I can hardly believe that I am almost ninety years old! It seems like only yesterday that I was thirteen, getting off the ship in Brooklyn and amazed by the thousands of tall buildings.

So much has transpired in my life, good and bad. I do not know how or when my life will end—that is the mystery of life, we don't know how much of life we will get. My Susan got sixty-nine years only. My mother lived to be ninety-two. My family members murdered in the Holocaust were as young as sixteen years old.

The fact is, nobody knows how long they will live. During our lives, however long or short they may be, we all have many obligations and responsibilities and we cannot always control what comes our way. But we also have many choices that we can make about who we want to be and how we want to spend our time.

•◦•

I used to put pictures on Facebook now and again but not too often. The trouble is, I would simply forget about Facebook and then when I did remember to check, there were so many messages and comments, I could hardly keep up with it. It was overwhelming. There was a time when I would argue with people about politics on Facebook, but it got me too worked up. I didn't want to spend time arguing with people I have never met, and these arguments seemed never to end and just make everybody upset and angry.

I do like to watch television from time to time, but I do keep my eye out for how long I am watching it. Sometimes I say, "Gidon Lev, get up and do something else!" Also, television bombards me with too much, too fast. When I change the channels on the TV, trying to find a news program or even a travel show like *National Geographic*, which I love, I have to go through so many other channels that I find myself overwhelmed. Seeing all these programs thrown at me, I end up, sometimes, just closing it all off. Then I take a book or a newspaper and simply inform myself in a more casual and calm way by choosing what interests me and what I want to read about.

I do see and notice that many people spend a great deal of their time online. Sometimes I even notice people looking at their phones in restaurants or other situations when they are surrounded by plenty of people to speak to and interact with. This seems like a shame to me because we can miss opportunities to socialize, even if we are doing something boring like waiting in a line. There is always the possibility to take up a conversation with somebody and learn more about each other and about the world.

The problem with being constantly on the internet is that it becomes overly gripping. There is so much information online and so many other people, total strangers from all over the world with their social media comments and opinions, which are often very strong and overpowering. People spend a lot of time arguing with each other. An old Jewish proverb says that it's better to be smart than to be right, but I think not enough people have heard that one, because people keep arguing, sometimes for days, when it's smarter to do something productive!

It is truly a bit of a personal struggle to balance things out. Not everybody succeeds in doing that. You get so involved and so tied to something that you forget there is the rest of the world right outside your door, full of life and activity.

I will admit that sometimes I can get carried away with reading and find myself getting tired even though I am not doing anything. So I try to balance it out by opening the front door and taking myself for a short walk in the fresh air.

·•·

Julie and I make it a habit to spend time together walking on the trails out in nature. This is especially good for us when we need to relax from the stress that day-to-day life sometimes brings with it. One such day was spent hiking and exploring the Banias freshwater spring and waterfalls, where there are the ruins of an ancient shrine to the Greek god Pan that are over two thousand years old.

It is a bit of a hike down to the falls, but I managed it with the help of the walking stick my friend Itzhak made for me and just taking it slowly and enjoying the sights and sounds along the way.

When we reached the site of the ruins, we could see, carved into the rocks, an opening to a cave. I learned that the ancient Greeks believed that this was the entrance to Hades, where the fertility gods went in the winter only to come up in the spring and bring with them a hopeful new season and new life.

Two thousand plus years is a long time ago, and yet the same water is still flowing, which, in a way, brings the whole place to life once more. Being somewhere so ancient and so profound, with the water flowing all around me, makes me feel a part of history and of the universe. It puts many things in my life into a very clear and hopeful perspective.

After our wonderful hiking in nature and pondering of history, we went to one of our favorite little outdoor restaurants.

It is a very special place. A little stream runs right through the middle of it! There, they serve fresh trout, and it is delicious.

However, despite such a nice day and tasty lunch, somehow, on our way home, Julie and I had a disagreement. To be honest with you, I don't think either of us can remember what on earth we argued about, but as I recall we were both unhappy with the other. But there we were, stuck in the same car together, so we had to work it out.

As we drove along, we shared our feelings, and it turned out that Julie and I hadn't really been expressing ourselves to each other about our worries. We had been keeping our feelings deep inside and neither one of us realized how much of a toll that was taking on our ability to be patient with and understanding of each other, which is what led us to argue.

A good part of our grumpiness and lack of patience with each other was the result of our both being stressed out by the terrible situation surrounding us night and day—a war going on, with a great deal of suffering and angst and people being killed and displaced. Even though we try to watch over our mental health and not watch the news too much, this terrible situation surrounded us every day in ways large and small. The trouble was, we had not expressed that stress to each other.

During the long drive home, we delved into our deepest selves and were honest about how we were feeling. When we did this, we were able to see each other more clearly and compassionately. We were able to comfort each other and commiserate and even talk about our hopes for better days to come.

By the time we got home and finished our heartfelt conversation, we had both been reminded how important it is to talk about our feelings, good and bad, and that, of course, we still love each other very much.

Worrying and suffering and anxiety over things are not always evident, to ourselves or to others. Sometimes we simply try to adjust to our worries without knowing we are actually doing battle inside ourselves. But sometimes we do lose control over our emotions and the inevitable happens—we get upset and oftentimes at the very people for whom we care very much!

It would be a better, kinder world if all of us could be more aware of how we are feeling deep inside and learn to express ourselves honestly. But humans being human, we don't always do so. We keep ourselves too busy, rushing around to work and home and back again. We spend time online or watching television, but, in my opinion, we don't spend enough time thinking quietly and slowly about the most important things in life—who we truly are, who we want to be, and how remarkable the world around us really is.

•◆•

When I was younger and out in the fields or pastures with the cows, I sometimes liked to spend time observing the tiny world of ants. I enjoyed watching them lug things ten times their weight, working hard and creating their little world. Who knows, maybe ants also have wars and feasts and celebrations!

These days, I have become much more aware of the world of wings—birds of all sizes and colors, singing melodious sounds.

I can see birds of prey riding on the updrafts and going higher and higher as they look for their next meal. Sometimes I can see graceful white egrets and storks flying about in formation, with their long legs stuck out behind them.

It's something quite extraordinary to see a beautiful bird land on a branch so lightly and to notice the many different colors of his feathers and wonder where he will fly off to next. At times like this, I am amazed at the complexity and majesty of life.

I have no doubt that some of the birds that I see swooping over or around our enclave on the hill are part of the Hula Valley bird population, which is about an hour north of where I live. Many people may not know this, but this land of Israel is part of a very important migration route for millions and millions of birds of many species, from Europe to Africa and back again, twice a year. The Hula Valley is a gathering place for them along the way, so birdwatchers from all over the world like to go there and look at the birds with their binoculars.

•◆•

My late wife, Susan, was a writer and a poet both at heart and in practice, and she loved the Hula Valley very dearly. There, many a time did we camp and walk for long hours on the paths and over the bridges.

After Susan left us, my youngest son, Asher, gathered a number of her poems and made them into a book for us all to have and to cherish. One of my favorite poems that Asher chose to include is about good intentions. Susan called this poem "To Gidon—The Question."

To Gidon—The Question

What mischief have I done
Poking around in your heart?

Soliciting love for a worthy cause
Giving it mostly on my terms,

Irrigating deserts and
Thinning forests, building roads

Digging canals and yet
Hoping to be ecologically friendly?

Are you my beloved Hula Valley
Where I drained swamps only

To realize the damage done
And flood them again years later?

Have I been kind enough
To your water buffaloes and wild boars?

Can love settle in a landscape
But also leave it intact?

You see, at times, Susan felt that perhaps her insistence that we, the members of our family, and me especially, express ourselves may have been overly zealous. In this poem, she related our sometimes stormy relationship to the land in the Hula Valley and the changes it went through.

I wish I could tell Susan that she did not damage my heart or my soul; in fact, she helped me to be more expressive and self-aware and I will always be grateful to her for that. The fact is, she is one of the reasons I am able to share so much of myself today!

But it is true that the Hula Valley, which used to be a big swampy, marshy place, was totally changed with the best of intentions and that change harmed the balance of nature in many ways. Before all this, the land in the Hula Valley was not usable (or so we humans thought!) and mosquitoes carrying malaria bred there, causing a great deal of sickness and even death in the nearby villages.

Sometime in the 1950s, it was decided to improve the Hula Valley by draining most, but not all, of the swamp in order to add agricultural land to many of the struggling farms and villages. But this change, which was seen at the time as a big improvement, caused many unforeseen consequences. There was a balance of nature before, and the ecosystem and everything in it—the birds, fish, frogs, insects, and even the water snakes—depended on their natural conditions and could not survive a man-made change that was so drastic. The bird migrations stopped coming to the Hula Valley and the soil, used to being underwater, was so dry it just blew away in the air.

Though the Hula Valley was, in many places, muddy and messy and difficult to get around, it simply had to be restored. It took almost forty years and a lot of work, but in the end, the wetlands were flooded again and the natural balance of the Hula Valley was restored. In fact, it was even improved upon because wooden walkways were installed in many of the marshes so people could spend time in this peaceful place. The walkways are low so that you can walk along quietly and not disturb the wildlife, especially the birds, who often nest down close to the ground and hide in the reeds.

·•·

Life is full of unexpected ups and downs. Sometimes even in one day. The best, most well-intentioned plans sometimes don't work out the way we think they will. Anything can happen. This is the way this crazy life is—unpredictable. The fact is, try as we might, there's very little we can actually control, so it helps to simply be open-hearted and allow ourselves to be the complicated humans that we are. After all, it's only human to sometimes feel downhearted or to worry or to have regrets.

But there is always tomorrow and that's what gives me hope. Being hopeful isn't always easy because it means we have to be aware of what is going on around us, what is on our minds, how we are truly feeling. It is much easier not to do that, believe me! I wasn't always as aware of my feelings and emotions and I didn't always have my priorities straight about what is important to me, although life always had a way of reminding me. But I wouldn't be me if I hadn't gone through so many experiences, good and bad, from the lowest lows to the highest highs. All these moments in my life have contributed to who I am today and I think I'm a pretty decent guy!

Being self-aware is not always pleasant—of course we all get in bad moods and are daunted by worries or challenges. But we can accept ourselves as we are and still imagine something better in our own lives or even in the world. When you look around, most things that we humans have accomplished have come from imagining something better even in the darkest of times.

When I feel downhearted, I give myself some time to mull things over. Our minds can be very busy places, with a lot of traffic jams going on, so I take my attention off whatever I am worried about and free my mind to be creative and imaginative.

For example, if I simply take a few moments and look out of my windows, I can see a beautiful panorama of the valley and the hills surrounding it. I try to really notice the green fields and the gold hills and even the blue sky and the shapes of the constantly moving clouds.

When I step outside, I can breathe in the scent of the wild rosemary that grows everywhere, and I can reach down and find the smooth brown acorns that have fallen from the Mount Tabor and Cyprus oak trees. If I listen, I can hear and sometimes even see jackals yipping, and if I look up, there are always birds of every kind darting, singing, and swooping. All these things seem bigger to me than whatever I might be worrying about. It feels good to have my feet on the ground. I have never taken nature and its wonders for granted. I feel safe and free in the bosom of a forest or field of ripe corn or just ordinary winter wheat. For me, it is a way to soothe my soul and feel more at peace. It's like recharging my batteries so I can think more clearly about what is truly important to me—here and now.

I take care of my mind, body, and soul by spending time doing things that are enjoyable and good for me, like swimming at the community center, going to a musical concert, or just going outside to watch the birds for a while. I make sure to spend time with the people I love, face-to-face, or talking on the phone and sharing with each other our hopes and dreams and also our troubles and challenges. I look at art books or go to museums as often as I can. When I happen to see an art gallery here or there, I am sure to stop by and have a look for a few minutes. Sometimes I might even make art, even if it's something simple like painting chairs with *Hope* and *Joy* written on them. I notice little kids playing and ants building and the way the clouds change shape as they sail by.

There are many more positive things, large and small, happening all around us than bad things. You will notice this if you pay attention. It might not always seem like it, but we each have a choice as to which aspects of life we focus on. Teach yourself to pay attention to what you pay attention to. Sometimes you have to take it one day at a time or even an hour at a time. In the end, it really is possible to choose to notice what is good, even something small, and to use your imagination and creativity and be hopeful for a better future.

14

SAYING YES TO HOPE

Gidon in 2023.

IN THERESIENSTADT, THE ARTISTIC PERFORMANCES, THE ORCHESTRAS and theater and puppet shows, while they lasted, were important and good for us prisoners. It gave us a sense of being human because we were being creative and active. We were doing and enjoying things that we loved.

But it wasn't only artistic endeavors that helped us feel more human and have a tiny sense of normalcy at Theresienstadt; ordinary things did too. Of course, Theresienstadt was anything but ordinary, but somehow, in our minds, we had to make it so. Sweeping or cleaning even a tiny corner of a crowded room, sewing and repairing garments, washing out our cups and bowls, trying to stay clean—these small activities of life reminded us that we were human, our lives mattered, and tomorrow was a possibility and maybe even another tomorrow after that.

Throughout my life, that feeling of determination and even defiance has stayed with me. For me, each day is filled with challenges, some daunting and some less so; however, I welcome this challenge called life! No matter what life throws at me, as long as I am doing something, even something very ordinary, I feel that I am somehow saying: I am here! I am alive!

•◆•

To me, food is anything but ordinary. When I was in Theresienstadt, food was something that I was lucky to have even one or two mouthfuls of, no matter what it was. I needed the sustenance to keep going for another day. I was so little when I first went to the camp that I didn't really have memories of normal food except one from before the war: my mother and I having lunch with one of my great aunts in Prague and she served kaiser rolls, which I loved. I remember reaching for another one and my mother kicked me under the table! As I recall, I managed to sneak a roll out in a napkin anyway.

•◆•

There was an instance of some women at Theresienstadt, who, after work, late into the night, somehow gathered together to share and write down some of their favorite recipes. These, they hoped one day, when all this horror was over, they could once again make for their families in their kitchens. These women wrote down all sorts of recipes, for rich, buttery cakes, crusty fruit pies, and delicious meats and thick stews with Czech spices. Of course, this was wishful thinking and dreaming, but it lifted their spirits and gave them hope.

Somehow these women were never caught doing this and they managed to put their recipes together into a book and bind it with some thread. This cookbook somehow survived the war, but it took decades before it was sent to one of the descendants of the women who wrote it.

I can only imagine what it felt like to see that cookbook, written under such conditions. In fact, it was discovered when the recipes were translated that some of the recipes were lacking in some basic ingredients or had confusing or mixed-up directions. This breaks my heart. The women who undertook to make this cookbook were suffering from such terrible conditions of starvation, illness, and fear that they made a lot of mistakes. But they did their best. To me, this is one of the most beautiful yet sad stories of Theresienstadt.

I don't believe my mother was a part of the creation of that cookbook, but in the testimony she wrote about her time in Theresienstadt, she said that she shared a room for a while with a woman to whom she read recipes aloud. My mother wrote that just looking at the recipes so rich with butter and eggs was like a dream to her. My mother kept this cookbook she read aloud from, and I remember it well. I believe my uncle Gustav must have given his treasured cookbook to my mother for safekeeping when he and his wife, Dora, were sent to Auschwitz from Theresienstadt. Many years later, I gave this cookbook to my cousins in New York and they have it to this day.

•–•

When the kids were growing up, Susan did the cooking, and she was a wonderful cook. Her Spaghetti Bolognese is still legendary in our family and nobody has been able to re-create it, though we have all tried. Susan's rule was that nobody was allowed in the kitchen when she was cooking. The kitchen was her kingdom!

I never really learned to cook, but in the past few years, I have gotten myself into the kitchen and given cooking a shot. In my opinion, I'm a pretty good cook. Of course, my favorite meal to make is chicken soup with homemade matzo balls, but I also make excellent, very creamy mashed potatoes that I like to serve with my Hungarian goulash with lots and lots of paprika. If Sue could see me now, she wouldn't believe it.

If I could have imagined, back when I was so hungry all the time in Theresienstadt, that today I can be creative in the kitchen and make whatever I want and eat as much as I want, I wouldn't have believed it. Somehow being in the kitchen, wearing my apron, with the radio on, listening to music, I feel very relaxed and creative. It helps me take my mind off other worries and to appreciate what I have and look forward to eating.

I enjoy shopping for food and spices and looking at recipes to try. There are many new recipes that I want to try in the future, including a Thai soup called Tom Kha Gai that I tasted at a restaurant not too long ago. For that, I have to get some special spices, though.

A couple of years ago, I was even invited to the test kitchen of Adeena Sussman, who has written a few very good cookbooks. Adeena wanted me to teach her how to make *knedlíky*. I was a bit nervous because there were a lot of cameras and people there filming and because I make *knedlíky* only from memory, so I don't know the exact measurements. But make it I did, and when it was done, I showed Adeena how to slice the tender, steaming *knedlíky* with a thread, the way my mother taught me. Afterward, we had some together, with some very good gravy Adeena had made, and it was delicious. I think she was impressed that this old guy can cook!

◆

Dancing, too, has always made me feel hopeful. For a short time in Canada, I thought I might become a professional dancer, but it didn't work out because I could not afford to take the necessary lessons.

The fact is, when I was living in Toronto, my mom, Jus, and I had very little money. For a while we lived with my mother's cousin. Jus was not yet working because he had just arrived and didn't speak English. Eventually, my mom got a job at a millinery shop downtown, and Jus found a job in a textile factory.

At that time, my heroes were Gene Kelly and Fred Astaire. I admired their dancing very much. They were so graceful, handsome, strong, and elegant. I wanted to be like that too! I knew there was no chance I could take dance lessons, but

I wouldn't let that fact get in the way of what I wanted. So I looked around to see how I could make my own tap shoes.

I took some old shoes of mine and attached small metal heel protectors, front and back. Heel protectors were used at that time to extend the life of the soles of your shoes, but they also made the tapping sound that I so loved. They weren't exactly what Gene Kelly wore, but I was thrilled. That was step one. Then I had to learn how to do some steps. We had an old record player, so I bought myself a couple of Gene Kelly records at a used record store.

Then, in the quietness of my room, when my mother and Jus were at work, I put on the record and I copied the sounds that I heard on the record, tap by tap. I didn't have a mirror to look in to see how I was doing, I only had the sound. I seemed to have a knack for it, but nobody ever saw me dance until sixty-seven years later!

On my eighty-second birthday, my daughter Hadasa gave me a brand-new pair of tap-dance shoes. They were the first ones I had ever owned and they were so perfect and beautiful. I still sometimes put them on and just walk around my house to hear them click. Every few steps I do a little jig!

Hadasa is quite a dancer herself, and she was part of a tap-dance group. She encouraged me to join and take some lessons too. I was a little hesitant about the lessons, not being sure that I could keep up. There were many other people in our group, young and old, of every different size and shape, and somehow I felt that this old guy could do it too, and that I did!

In my very last performance with the group, when I was eighty-five, we did a tap-dance performance at the community center, and the place was packed. Of course, my kids and friends came and the families of the other members of our dance class. We wore dark costumes with a red sequined tie. The lights came on and out we went, the whole of us. We did a tap performance to "Up a Lazy River" and we made it all the way through and got a standing ovation!

•••

I never did like the idea of retiring, but a couple of years ago, I finally had to throw in the towel. Until I was eighty-seven years old, I kept busy delivering flowers for three brothers who owned three different florist shops in my neighborhood. For some unknown reason to me, they were not on speaking terms with each other, although they were actually located not far from each other. Sometimes it rubbed off on me. When one of the brothers called me to come and deliver, I'd have to point out that Yaacov called before Yitzhak and therefore I had to deliver for Yaacov first and Yitzhak second. One time, they had me deliver to the same neighborhood—houses next door to each other—but I didn't know because they didn't talk, so I made two trips.

Believe me, this job was not so easy. Most of my deliveries were in a very old neighborhood where the markings on the buildings and apartments were not updated or clear. The buildings and streets are all jumbled together.

Sometimes I went up three flights of steps with big, heavy bouquets of flowers only to find I was in the wrong building or the wrong floor. This was challenging, to put it mildly. As far as parking was concerned, it was very hard to find, so I made a little sign and put it on my car: I AM A FLOWER DELIVERY MAN AND I WILL BE BACK VERY SOON.

I did get, from time to time, parking fines, but when I got a parking ticket, I would usually challenge it and ask for a court date. At the court, seeing that I am elderly, they usually were lenient with their decisions and they almost always reduced my fines.

One time, a lady judge said, "Mr. Lev, I know you are an old gentleman, but please stop getting all these tickets. Maybe you should stop working in this field because I'm sure the money you make can't possibly pay the parking fines even if I reduce them. After all, you're no longer a spring chicken!"

One time, I made a delivery to a rabbi. I was about to leave when he stopped me and told me to wait. He brought me a tip, and as he was doing so, he said that I should know that it is a *mitzvah* (blessing) to give a tip to the person who delivers flowers. From that time on, when I delivered flowers to a religious home, without hesitation I would point out to them that it is a *mitzvah* to give me a tip, and it worked!

On Fridays, which were the busiest days all week, I would have five or six orders of flowers at a time all crammed in the back seat of my car. After a while, Julie insisted on helping me out on Fridays to make it easier and even enjoyable. On these busiest days, whether a Friday or a holiday, Julie and I would stop and have a falafel or a shawarma to rejuvenate us and give us energy to continue. The brothers who owned the florist shops got used to seeing Julie come along on Fridays and always told me how lucky I am, which is true. Julie also learned some off-color Hebrew words from them!

In the end, it became a little bit too hard to run up three of four flights of steps, not to mention dealing with the traffic and parking. Finally, at the age of eighty-seven, I came to the conclusion that enough was enough. My employers were not happy with my departure because, it turned out, they really depended on me and I did a good job. There was not one occasion when I didn't find the address to deliver the flowers. But the brothers accepted my decision because they had no choice.

To this day, when I pass by one of the shops, they are very friendly and ask me if I am ready to deliver to a couple of places. I laugh and say, "No thank you, Avraham, no thank you, Yitzhak, no thank you, Yaacov—thank you, but no thank you!"

•◆•

There was a time in my life when my philosophy of "here and now" and always keeping busy backfired on me. Especially during my first bout with cancer, my "here and now" was miserable. I didn't have the energy to do anything. I had no appetite, no plans, nothing to look forward to, and nowhere to be—except another chemotherapy treatment. My chemotherapy treatments, which were supposed to make me better (they eventually did), made me feel worse and worse. There was a cumulative effect of drained energy and hopelessness, and there was nothing I could do about it.

You see, when I was in Theresienstadt, I was hungry all the time, but I had the ability to go outside and try to find a bite of food. If I was cold, I could try to gather wood and get warmer. There were small things I could do to try to feel better. There were small things that gave me hope.

When I was sick with cancer, I didn't feel I could do any-
thing, large or small. I felt hopeless. Every day felt like a long,
dark cloudy day that would never end. I could not see a future,
feeling this way. But it was still there if I could only imagine it.
I needed help.

I credit Susan for helping me to imagine a future when I
felt like giving up. She was scared and maybe a bit angry to see
me so hopeless. So she made a list of things I would miss if I
gave up. I wouldn't see our daughter graduate, I wouldn't see
our son get married—and so on. She painted a picture of our
future as a family and said, "So, what, you're going to give up
on all that, Gidon? After everything we have done and been
through?"

It was that talking to, showing me a future that I wanted to
be a part of, that kept me going for one more day. And then
one more day after that. And then another. Getting through
each day became the most that I could do. But that was some-
thing, and it started to add up, and finally, I did start feeling
better. But it took a long time.

Throughout most of my life, staying active, doing and cre-
ating, and working were the forms that hope took in my life.
But when I was sick, I learned another approach: simply being
able to imagine tomorrow is in and of itself a way to keep hope
alive within us.

•◆•

I am not prepared to near the end of my life without staying
busy and without hope for the future, so until this very day I
try to fix, clean, set up, and make things, large and small, more

efficient, more orderly, more presentable. It simply makes my life nicer and more enjoyable. I admit that my way of thinking is not for everyone, but to me, there is a lot to be said for keeping up a routine every day and doing all sorts of small things to make our lives nicer. Whether it's raking the lawn or trying a new recipe, everything we do that is active, that moves our bodies, that engages us says, "Yes, there will be a tomorrow!"

15

LET'S MAKE THINGS BETTER

Gidon and Julie in 2021.

Gidon and Julie in New York City in 2020.

"IF THINGS ARE NOT AS YOU WISH, WISH THEM AS THEY ARE."

When I first read this Yiddish proverb, late in my life, I simply could not understand it.

On that cold, wintry day on December 14, 1941, when I arrived at the entrance to Theresienstadt, I was cold, exhausted, and frightened. I wanted my red tricycle and I wanted very badly to be with my loving grandpa and my father. I wished I was back home in Karlovy Vary. But this was not the reality for me on that terrible day nor would it ever be again. How could I possibly ever wish things to be as they were then, in Theresienstadt, much less the days, weeks, months, and years that came after, with its deprivation, suffering, and fear?

There's no question that this terrible period certainly played a very big part in shaping my personality and outlook on life. At Theresienstadt, we all—men, women, young and old, and even us kids—had very little of anything. We had to make use of whatever we had, whether it was a scrap of food or cloth, a pencil or a button—any small thing to help us survive for another day and have even a tiny bit of hope. To this very day, I still try to be as resourceful as is humanly possible in all ways. I take a lot of pleasure in small accomplishments, and I always, always believe things can be even a tiny bit better.

For sure, I am not happy—to put it extremely mildly—about the way I went through my childhood. It was excruciatingly difficult and outright scary. The fact is, for the most part, effectively, I hardly had a childhood at all.

Of course, at the center of my sorrow was the loss, first and foremost, of my father and Grandpa Alfred, whom I loved so dearly. But today, all that is left for me is to accept what happened because I cannot change it. But I do have a very strong feeling that both my dad and my grandpa would be very proud of me for the way I not only survived but also managed to use the lessons that I learned during that time to make my life better.

•◆•

When I first went to Brooklyn with my mother in 1948, my life became a thousand percent better and different from what it had been in the concentration camp. First and foremost, I wasn't hungry all day every day. I also had a clean bed, warm clothes, and could walk around freely without fear. Those things made my new life almost like paradise. But I still wasn't satisfied. Walking on the streets, I saw diners and soda shops full of people enjoying delicious hamburgers, chips, hot dogs, and ice cream floats—chocolate and strawberry—I, too, wanted one of those ice cream floats! But I could only look in the window from the street because I didn't have money to buy anything.

There had to be a way to overcome this, so I took stock of the situation: Here I was, a thirteen-year-old kid who did not yet speak English, but I was free and I was independent. I had my legs, my arms, and my head. I looked and asked until I found myself a job delivering laundry. I didn't get paid, only tips, sometimes as much as a quarter, which was a lot of money then. Before long, I earned enough tip money to afford an ice cream soda. And I was thrilled! It was so good, I remember the taste of it to this day—strawberry. I had not only succeeded in making things a tiny bit better for one day but also boosted my belief in myself in my new country.

When I think about something that I want, whether that is an ice cream soda or something much more ambitious and complicated, I look around at what I already have that can help me. This I learned from my childhood.

I managed to do this even during one of the hardest times in my life, after Susan died. I had sold our family home and moved to a different part of Israel to be closer to my children. I didn't know what to do with myself. I needed to keep busy, but I was seventy-seven years old already. It was a real identity crisis for me, not having Susan and not knowing what I could do to keep busy. My kids were grown and I was on my own much sooner than I would have ever imagined.

But I did have a car and I had time. So I started looking around until I found that flower delivery shop and I asked them if I could deliver flowers, thinking that would help me get to know the place and maybe even meet some people that I wouldn't ordinarily meet. And that I did. Then the other brother hired me, and the third one too! I wound up being very busy!

So, finally, in some way, I think that I do understand the quote that if things aren't as you wish, you can wish them as they are. Because sometimes the way things are can give you new ideas and strengthen you, and can even be a factor in making you more resilient and creative.

Even though it is hardly easy, if we look around in our lives, we can find the things that we do possess that can help us feel better, do better, and maybe even make things better for others. When I delivered flowers, I made the world a little better for the people who received them, and that made me feel very good.

Too few of us notice what we actually *do* have already. That might be a roof over your head, even one good friend, your imagination, curiosity, and creativity, and even a simple determination and desire to be happier. If you can imagine that things can be better, you can make it so. You have the power within yourself to change your situation or the environment and even change and heal your own soul. That, in my opinion, is key.

My situation as a child—and not just me, but millions of others—was extreme, but many people go through sometimes long periods of life suffering for one reason or another. Illness can lead to permanent disability or even death. There is poverty; there is violence and pain, whether physical or emotional, and all of that makes life quite difficult and challenging. I think it's important to be able to feel empathy for others. It doesn't diminish you or your suffering but actually helps you and is good for your soul.

I do find it difficult seeing how people have so little empathy for each other. Is that more so today than earlier? I'm not sure, but I'm perhaps more conscious of it and therefore I try to go out of my way to engage more freely with others. Not always do I get a positive response, but just trying makes me feel that I'm having a positive effect.

For example, right now, my old friend Yaacov is suffering from chemotherapy treatments. A few times each week, I go over to his house and sit with him and we talk. When I was going through chemotherapy, it was so important to have people take an interest and talk to me, not necessarily about my illness but about all sorts of things.

Sometimes the problems in our lives and certainly in the world can be overwhelming and totally discouraging. It is very difficult to imagine things getting better, even as much as we would love for them to be. Our situation today is daunting, to put it mildly. We can hardly see the light at the end of the tunnel.

You might think that you as an individual can do very little to effect a change. For example, I am not a rich person or a politician or a well-known world leader. I'm just Gidon Lev, an everyday guy who has, many times in my life, tried to make things better.

I think it was Yaacov who told me about a quote by Rabbi Tarfon, who lived a very, very long time ago: "You are not obligated to complete the work, but neither are you free to abandon it."

Some people think that the rabbi means, essentially, that there is always a lot of work to do, and there is also always a limited time to do it in, whether that is an hour, a day, a week, or even our whole lives. Our work is seemingly never done, which is why this saying makes a lot of sense to me. I used to be a kind of workaholic when I was younger, and I admit that this lingers with me today. But I don't think that Rabbi Tarfon was talking about that kind of work.

I wanted to understand more about this saying, so I used Google and found a parable about a king who hires workers to fill in a giant hole. One worker looks at it and says, "This is too big. I can never finish this!" Another worker says, "I was hired for only a day. At least I have a job!"

I like that parable because it focuses on the here and now. It focuses on what one individual can do, depending on their attitude and outlook. To me, "the work" that Rabbi Tarfon talks about is like a job, and this job is improving things. So, of course, we cannot stop trying because that would mean we are giving up. We can't give up because striving, doing, hoping, loving, and creating are the essence of our being human and, when you think about it, of life itself!

•◆•

Though sometimes it doesn't seem like it, life itself is truly a gift, and we should hold onto it and grasp it with both hands. In all my mortal existence, I have never received a phone call or text message from someone who has passed away telling me what they are doing now that they are dead!

Of course I am saddened that there is so much suffering and pain all over the world. For many years, I certainly wasn't aware of what life was like in places that were far away from me or the different problems in those places. Now, with so much media and information, I am much more aware of the difficulties that so many millions of people face. Things like wars, diseases, famines, and more. Especially today, the world, in many places and instances, truly seems to have gone haywire. If there was any way that I could make things better, I would do so immediately, but I sometimes don't know what I can do to help. I think that's the same for so many of us.

For a while, Julie and I did work as volunteers at a food distribution center in Ramat Gan. Mostly it was me, actually. Julie came when she wasn't writing or working. This organization collected donations of food from restaurants, cafés, and grocery stores. Either the food had not sold or was aging and not fresh, but it was still perfectly edible.

A dozen or so of us volunteers would put on aprons and gloves and start by sorting the food and organizing it into categories such as meat, hot dishes, baked goods, and fruits and vegetables. Then we arranged parcels to be delivered by other volunteers to the homes of needy families and citizens of our town. It was a very fulfilling activity, especially when we also got to deliver these donations to actual homes and were the recipients of the joyful faces and thankfulness!

I am very happy that I was able to be part of this project as my small way of contributing to making our society better. We volunteers were not the only ones to take part in such a project; many such organizations all over the world help distribute food. But I am quite convinced there are not enough.

Maybe it is because I never had enough food to eat when I was small, but to me it is totally unacceptable and there is no excuse that restaurants, grocery stores, and even private homes throw away so much food every day. Tons and tons of perfectly good food that people really need goes into the garbage. This must and will change in the near future. After all is said and done, there is more than enough food for us all, especially if we eliminate the waste and work together to get this food to the people who need it.

Of course, everybody has something near and dear to them that can also match up with their talents, skills, and passions. For example, Julie is very good at giving speeches and talks and she's also very good with people. She has a way of making people feel comfortable and good, especially young people. So she has spent a lot of time doing volunteer work right here in Israel and in the West Bank, helping young entrepreneurs to express themselves and their ideas with confidence so they can be more successful in their careers. One time, she taught a whole class of survivors from the massacres in Darfur in

Sudan how they could make their own websites to help them find better jobs. I was very proud of her!

My grandson Eshel is an agronomist, and he spent several years in Ethiopia working for a nonprofit organization to improve agriculture so that farmers could grow better crops, get out of poverty, and not suffer from malnutrition. Ethiopia is where Eshel met my lovely granddaughter-in-law Reut, and they had a beautiful wedding in the Arava Desert a few years ago. Now they have their own farm there. The NGO Eshel worked for helped provide Ethiopian farmers with better-quality seeds and taught them new ways to care for their crops. Eshel and Reut spent time in the fields working, teaching, explaining, and making things better in small yet significant ways. I was and am so proud and thankful that I have such a grandson and granddaughter-in-law who are doing such important work.

For me, to imagine the difference that Eshel, Reut, Julie, and so many others like them have made, person by person, one at a time, is overwhelming.

My son Yanai, Eshel's father, went to Rwanda in 2023 together with two or three other volunteers. There, he and the others taught acrobalance and juggling skills to street children. Yanai was there for about a week. He and his friends gave those children something very special that they never thought they could do, and it made those kids feel good, brought them together, and gave them a sense of joy and hope for a better future. Who knows what that might inspire in those kids in the future.

My son Shaya, who works at Hebrew University, studies the way pain works so that in the future we can help those with chronic pain be better understood and feel better. My daughter Hadasa helps design cities so that people can be more social and connected. My son Asher teaches people how the art of dance can free their souls, my daughter Maya teaches yoga to help people be more connected to their spirits, and my son Elisha helps ship goods all around the world so that people get what they need.

It makes me so happy and hopeful when I think about how my kids and so many hundreds of thousands of people do things like this all over the world every day. These are people choosing to be helpful and hopeful when they could be worried, angry, or sad. By doing what they can and participating in such activities, they are choosing to help make things better for us all instead of giving up or turning too far inward and focusing on themselves only.

Change comes from the bottom up, one person at a time. When one person does something positive, that connects them to other people, and you can get a strong momentum going. You can also have momentum in the opposite, and negative, direction, and I'm afraid there is much too much of that today. But I truly believe that change will come. I think things are changing right now because even when—especially when—things are not so good, that is when people take notice and start to change.

In today's world we are very much encouraged to think of ourselves as individuals. A great deal of emphasis is given to the individual, especially the young. In my day, this focus on individuals was not something that many people gave a lot of thought to. This is good, in many ways, because we are unique individuals and our thoughts, feelings, and experiences do matter, sometimes very much so. I wish that had been the case when I was a kid, after liberation. But it was not to be at that time.

But today, we have possibly gone too far toward thinking of our individual selves. So much so that many young people are quite separated or isolated from their friends, their communities, and even their own families. They are often totally self-absorbed, yet at the same time they are probably quite lonely. They seem to be drifting and searching for some meaning or purpose.

Especially during challenging times, we cannot sit on the side, so to speak, and not get engaged. If you don't feel a sense of purpose, just take a look around. Everywhere you look, help is needed. Surely, you will find many a place where you can be helpful and engaged, which in the end helps you feel hopeful because you are making a difference, even a small one, in your own way. That in itself is very satisfying.

I never saw myself as a person with a mission or a purpose. I never looked at my life in that way. But for me, the very opportunity of writing this book has given me a strong sense of purpose and that actually helps me to feel more connected to you, my community, and the world at large.

.•.

Sometimes people don't always want to hear the opinions and thoughts of an ordinary old guy. But writing this book for you to read has allowed me to explore so many of my memories and experiences on a much deeper level. It also gave me the chance to look back on my life in ways that I rarely have done before. I have learned a great deal more about the world, my life in the past, and even more importantly, my life in this present state. I have even looked deeper into my heart and soul to ask what is really important to me, here and now, at this stage of my life. I have learned a tremendous lot, and I imagine that if my Susan were around, she would be amazed at how much introspection I am now able to do!

Julie and I had long conversations and talks as we worked on this book together, and it seemed very natural and important to me to think about and consider not just my own life but also life in the bigger sense. Every day as we worked, I sat in my favorite yellow chair. It's the same one that I sat in when Susan told me not to be alone. I think Susan would be pleased that I am still alive and happy today, have found such a loving partner as Julie, and am reflecting deeply on my life, the way she always encouraged me to do.

I am hopeful that when you, my dear reader, pick up this book, you will find a connection not only between you and me but also with your family, friends, and the world at large. Perhaps in reading about my struggles and adventures, you, too, will find the courage and wherewithal to venture out and try something new and different that will give you a new lease on life and hope. Never be afraid to look or seem ridiculous because that's part of being human.

Perhaps reading and seeing how, at times, it was so hard for me to overcome adversities (some even of my own making!), you will be encouraged not to give up. And that is a victory for us all. Because you just might inspire somebody else, and they may follow your lead and do the same. And that can change the world and make this a better place for all of us.

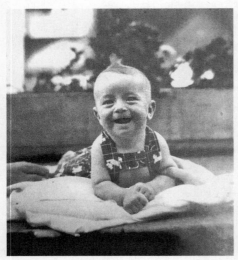

Gidon, circa 1935.

Gidon at age three, circa 1938.

The pendant Gidon's father, Ernst, gave his mother, Doris, the day he was sent to Auschwitz.

Gidon's mother, Doris, and his stepfather, Jus, circa 1950.

(*Left to right*) Gidon's grandmother Alice (Eliška) and Gidon's mother, Doris, circa 1917.

(*Left to right*) Gidon's grandmother, Theresie; his father, Ernst; Gidon; and his grandfather, Alfred, circa 1940–1941.

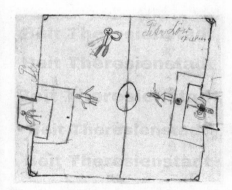

The drawing Gidon made in Theresienstadt, circa 1943.

Gidon in 1959.

Gidon at Purim in 2020.

Gidon visiting Karlovy Vary in 2021.

Gidon at the building where his family took refuge in Prague in 1938. This is where the Stolpersteine will be placed in September 2024.

(*Left to right*) Gidon's grandson, Ido; Gidon's son, Shaya; and Gidon holding a photo of his father, Ernst.

ACKNOWLEDGMENTS

To my wonderful children, Maya, Yanai, Hadasa, Shaya, Asher, and Elisha—I am very proud and lucky to be your *aba*. Thank you for being such unique, creative, expressive human beings and thank you for my wonderful grandchildren (and great-grandchildren!) and, mostly, thank you for putting up with your crazy dad!

To my dear family and friends, near and far, who in one way or another have been a part of my life, I am forever thankful and appreciative to each one of you beyond the words that I can possibly write here.

So many thanks to all those of you, from all over the world, who have followed me on social media and let me know in very loving ways that I have encouraged you and given you hope—and sometimes even made you laugh! Your love and support mean a lot to me and have kept me dancing.

Of course, I want to also thank our agents Richard Pike at C&W and Eric Lupfer at UTA for believing in this book from day one and giving it their all in every way. Thank you to our editor at Hachette, Renee Sedliar, for being so warm, encouraging, and patient with Julie and me both, all along the way. The fact is, you made writing this book fun!

Thanks are due also to my late wife, Susan Deborah Lev, who may, at this very moment, be looking down and smiling.

Acknowledgments

I am grateful for her love and insights, poetry and patience with me for more than forty years.

Most importantly, I want to thank Julie, my best friend, love, and life partner, who not only taught me so much about writing, caring, and creativity but also listened to my meanderings and encouraged me to be expressive of myself and my feelings. Thank you, Julie, for taking a chance on this old man and going on this adventure with me. You have made my later years very special!

ABOUT THE AUTHOR

Gidon Lev was born Petr Wolfgang Löw in 1935 in Karlovy Vary (Carlsbad) in the Czech Republic. He was deported to the Theresienstadt concentration camp north of Prague in 1941 at the age of six and remained in the camp until liberation in May 1945. Married twice, Gidon is the father of six, with fifteen grandchildren and two great-granddaughters. He now lives in Northern Israel with his life partner of many years, Julie Gray.

·—•·

Julie Gray was born in 1964 in the San Joaquin Valley in California and grew up in Mount Shasta. In 2012, she moved to Tel Aviv and founded the Tel Aviv Writer's Salon. Julie's writing can be found in *The Times of Israel*, *Moment magazine*, *HuffPost*, *The Jewish Journal of Greater Los Angeles*, the *New York Post*, and many other publications. A passionate believer in the power of storytelling, Julie has volunteered with the Afghan Women's Writing Project, the Middle East Peace Initiative, the United States Agency for International Development, Kids for Peace, and Amnesty International. In 2017, Julie met Gidon Lev and has been writing and creating content about his story of hope ever since.